To Bill Cohen —

We've been waiting a long
time, but here it is!

Enjoy & good health
to you.

Richie Holand
12/5/83

THE
FOOD
SENSITIVITY
DIET

THE
FOOD
SENSITIVITY
DIET

DOUG A. KAUFMANN
with
RACQUEL SKOLNIK

Freundlich Books
New York

Published by Freundlich Books
80 Madison Avenue
New York, New York 10016

Distributed to the trade by
The Scribner Book Companies, Inc.

Manufactured in the United States of America

10   9   8   7   6   5   4   3   2   1

Library of Congress Cataloging in Publication Data
Kaufmann, Doug A., 1949-
The food sensitivity diet.
Bibliography: p.
1. Food allergy—Diet therapy. 2. Food allergy—Diet
therapy—Recipes. I. Skolnik, Racquel, 1946-
II. Title
RC596.K38   1984   616.97′5   83-20524
ISBN 0-88191-003-1

The authors are grateful to the following for permission to reprint material:
From *Love Your Body* by Viktoras Kulvinskas
Published by 21st Century Publications, PO# 702 Fairfield, IA 52556.
From *Tracking Down Hidden Food Allergy* by William G. Crook, M.D., ©
1980, Professional Books, P.O. Box 3494, Jackson, TN 38301.
From the book *Brain Allergies, The Psycho-Nutrient Connection* by William
H. Philpott, M.D., and Dwight K. Kalita, Ph.D. © 1980 by the authors. Re-
printed with permission of Keats Publishing, Inc., New Canaan, CT (Dr. Phil-
pott is also author of *Victory Over Diabetes* with Dr. Kalita, Keats Publishing,
Inc.)
From *Anatomy of an Illness* by Norman Cousins. W.W. Norton & Company,
Inc. © 1979 by Company, Inc., New York, NY. Used by permission.
From Roger J. Williams, *Physician's Handbook of Nutritional Science*, ©
1978. Courtesy of Charles C. Thomas, Publisher, Springfield, Il.
From Lendon Smith, M.D., *Foods For Healthy Kids*, © 1981, McGraw-Hill
Book Company, New York, NY. Used by permission.
From Dr. C. Keith Connors, *Food Additives for Hyperactive Children*, ©
1980, Plenum Publishing Corp., New York, NY. Used by permission.

CONTENTS

PART II
THE FOOD SENSITIVITY DIET—
CUSTOMIZED UNIQUELY FOR EACH INDIVIDUAL

ACKNOWLEDGMENTS

Research scientists are the unsung heroes of medical advance. Their names rarely reach the public; yet the tedious, repetitious and painstakingly detailed work they do is at the core of every worthwhile medical breakthrough. One such scientist is Dr. Geoffrey Cheung, biochemist and immunologist, who is head of Research and Development at Physicians Laboratories.

When we first met, Geoff greeted my wide-eyed enthusiasm about Cytotoxic testing with a typical scientist's skepticism. But because he is also a visionary and dreamer, he was able to shrug off his initial cynicism, and that of his peers, and begin the task of unraveling the mysteries behind the Cytotoxic reaction.

We have always known, subjectively, that the elimination of food sensitivities has a profound effect on the healing process, but we didn't know what, biochemically, caused the reaction to occur. We still don't have all the answers, but the work of Dr. Cheung, whose insights abound throughout this book, has uncovered many of the biochemical interactions leading up to the Cytotoxic Effect.

Special acknowledgment must also go to the pioneering work done by Dr. T. K. Bryan and Marian Bryan, who developed the testing procedure we now use. Their continued research and development on the Cytotoxic Effect has played a major role in the growth of this field.

Throughout the history of Physicians Laboratories, I have been fortunate enough to work with some of the most innovative medical doctors and health care professionals i the world. A complete list would be endless, but I would like to especially thank pediatricians Jay Gordon and Paul Fleiss, orthomolecular psychiatrists Harvey Ross and Allen Cott, University of Southern California researcher Everett Hughes, holistic medical doctor Rob Krakovitz and bariatrician Milton Gotlib, M.D. for their invaluable assistance on various parts of this manuscript.

The editorial assistance provided by Colin Peno, who helped guide the work from beginning to end is much appreciated; and I'd also like to thank Sheila Nealon, our editor, organizer and troubleshooter at Freundlich Books for her intelligent decisions and enthusiastic interest in this work.

Of course, the more than 20,000 people who have taken the Cytotoxic Test at Physicians Laboratories deserve a special accolade. I am encouraged by their positive feedback and thankful that they continue to let us know that the Food Sensitivity Diet really works.

FOREWORD

For some years in my medical practice, which is nutritionally oriented—especially in relation to how food may affect thinking, mood, behavior, and numerous physical complaints—I had been frustrated in my attempts to help some people whose problems apparently went beyond my knowledge. While attending several medical conferences I was introduced to the concept of food allergies; not like the allergies I had been taught about in medical school, but allergies that were nevertheless capable of causing severe problems. Like most physicians introduced to new concepts, I flatly rejected the idea that foods, some of which were even healthy foods like whole grains and milk, were capable of causing the incapacitating physical, emotional, and mental conditions I had been observing. As I listened to my patients in the following years, my own attitude changed slowly from, "It's not possible" to "Perhaps there is something to this idea of food allergies."

Another problem was to confront me, however, because when I decided that there was validity in the concept that food intolerance could cause some symptoms, I was obligated to try to help my patients who I thought were exhibiting this problem. I spoke to physicians who had been dealing with food allergies, all of whom were generous in sharing their knowledge. Not too much investigation was necessary to determine that the diagnosis of food sensitivities, at that time, would have required office space I didn't have, office personnel I didn't have, and a great deal of extra time I didn't have. There was no quick, relatively accurate, relatively inexpensive way to diagnose food sensitivities. I took the most expedient way of handling these suspected cases by referring them to a very competent physician in a nearby community who had been doing this work. Later, about the same time my patients began to object to my referral because of the distance and the time they had to wait before having their first visit, I was introduced to the Cytotoxic test.

I don't remember who the person was, but he brought with him on his first visit the results of a Cytotoxic test. After establishing my ignorance about the test, I was able to find out that it was performed in a laboratory on one sample of blood, and the form indicated that more than 150 foods were tested. Since the laboratory was in the same city, I called it and within the week had a visit from a very knowledgeable, enthusiastic, and sincere young man, Doug Kaufmann. With his help and the indulgence of my patients, I went through a very easy and quick learning period in the use of the Cytotoxic test.

I was made aware of the limitations of the test and the arguments questioning its validity, but most of all I listened to my patients. It was here that I felt the value of the test was established. Not that everyone improved—there are no 100 percents in medicine—but I was able to see significant improvement in a high percentage of patients who were able to follow the strict dietary program based on the results of Cytotoxic testing.

The Cytotoxic test has fulfilled the criteria I was looking for: my own office did not have to be changed—no new rooms, personnel, equipment, or schedule changes; the test was easy

to administer—just one blood sample; it was relatively accurate and relatively inexpensive compared to other methods of
determining sensitivities; the results of the test could be incorporated quickly into a treatment program.

Doug Kaufmann has been responsible for introducing me to
an added dimension in my work that has allowed me, in many
instances, to help people help themselves improve the quality
of their lives. The personal satisfaction he has given me by allowing me to be a better physician is of immeasurable worth.
Through the pages of this book Doug Kaufmann offers others
what he has given to me.

Thank you, Doug.

HARVEY M. ROSS, M.D.

Hollywood, California
May 1983

INTRODUCTION

My fascination with allergies began in 1970, during my Navy stint in Vietnam. I became fixated on attaining every medical certification the Navy offered; and while I was learning and observing, I began to notice that many of my friends—all young, healthy, and well exercised—were suffering horribly from allergies.

I scoured my medical textbooks but could find little information on my friends' plight. I translated this lack of information as a sign that their illnesses were not serious. Yet there they were, day after day, swallowing dangerously huge quantities of decongestants and antihistamines and taking cortisone shots, all to give them some relief from their constant sneezing, itching, stomach aches, and the rest.

My curiosity was aroused, and I couldn't wait to get back to the States to begin a thorough investigation into the causes of these allergies. I took a job at an allergy clinic while attending classes and worked as a laboratory technician. I soon became as frustrated as I imagine was the good doctor who ran the clinic. The only help he could give his patients was either to desensitize them—which entailed a painful series of injections, sometimes lasting for years—or to give them various medicines that would curb their symptoms. In most cases, he was unable to treat the causes.

Sometimes his patients would react frighteningly to the intradermal test used to determine allergies. In this test, a small amount of the suspected allergen is inserted under the patient's skin and the patient is observed by a nurse or the doctor to see if he reacts. The intradermal test usually turns up a "wheal" of redness appearing on the skin if the patient is allergic to the substance. But some clinic patients' reactions were so severe that emergency hospitalization was required. The patients' immune systems completely collapsed after introduction of the allergen. Equally frustrating was the guesswork involved in trying to determine which allergen, out of the many possibilities, to test.

There simply had to be a better way. I began reading everything I could get my hands on, and in 1972, I read about a new testing procedure developed by a husband and wife research team, Dr. William T. K. Bryan and Marian P. Bryan. The Bryans were linking food sensitivities to allergy symptoms, an interesting prospect. They were studying Cytotoxic Allergy Testing at the Washington University School of Medicine in St. Louis and were offering courses on the subject. I signed up immediately and submitted to the test.

My Cytotoxic test, which was performed on a sample of my blood, showed that 48 of my favorite foods were killing white blood cells in my blood sample. I was astounded. I had been tested for a complete panel of 125 food substances; having reacted to 48 of them, this meant that about 40 percent of all the foods I routinely consumed actually had a toxic effect on my body!

I found the test results hard to accept. Sure, the white blood cells were exploding outside my body in a laboratory situation. But were they exploding inside my body when I ate those very same foods? We now feel confident that this is the case. However, many years ago I questioned this phenomenon. Even worse, the foods I loved and therefore consumed often (this was before I understood my food addictions and cravings) were the same foods that reacted on the Cytotoxic test. My statement ten years ago is one I now hear every day in our offices. "I can't follow this program. That is every food I ever eat!"

I now realize how illogical that thinking is, but at the time I thought there was nothing wrong with me. I came away from the Bryans' course thinking their process was of little or no value either to me or, more importantly, to the clinic where I worked. I decided, though, after encouragement from my family, at least to try eliminating these foods from my diet for a few weeks.

I started on what I now refer to as the "caveman diet," consisting of the kinds of foods primitive man would have gathered, hunted, and consumed—fresh fruits, fresh vegetables, fresh fish and meats—as those foods were allowable on my particular program.

Having just returned from the Navy, I thought my health was better than it had ever been in my life. However, I remember running 10K races and feeling run down for a couple of days following each race. I was athletically inclined and loved almost every sport, especially tennis and racquetball, but I recall that after playing I would always experience a low period.

Also, in college classes scheduled after lunch periods, I would invariably fall asleep while the teacher was lecturing. This may seem to be a minor symptom, but it was certainly a problem for me.

Since childhood I can remember a neuralgia-type pain running from my left hip down my left leg, sometimes affecting my left foot. As this pain was intermittent and never severe enough to hamper my walking, I simply lived with it. I now understand that the condition was sciatica. Though it's fairly common, its cause has not yet been medically determined.

A short time after returning from Vietnam I noticed a skin reaction under my arms, in the fold of my arms, and at the top of my legs. As time went on, the itching became unbearable. Finally I went to a doctor and was placed on a steroid drug, told that it was probably some condition I had picked up in Vietnam, and patted on the back.

The reason I mention these problems is that I was a healthy young man, eating well, according to my knowledge, and yet I had all these symptoms. I never correlated them with food. Neither did my doctors. Now I look back and realize that the products I was fueling my body with were directly contributing to my problems.

Today, I do not fall asleep when being lectured to. I don't have sciatica, and I have no adverse skin conditions on my body. By eliminating the foods the Cytotoxic test showed were toxic to me, I ended these bothersome afflictions. The Cytotoxic test opened a door for me. The root of my problems was isolated, identified, and permanently eliminated.

In the late 1970s, I began Physicians Laboratories, Inc., of California to offer the Cytotoxic test to doctors and other health professionals and to conduct extensive research into the Cytotoxic effect. Our findings have confirmed many of our original suspicions. We have extracted blood from sick people and from ostensibly well people, and not once has any test been completely free of reactions. We *all* have food sensitivities. We don't all have food allergies.

The most fascinating part of this whole phenomenon is that what is toxic to me is not toxic to you. After performing more than twenty thousand Cytotoxic tests in our laboratories and seeing that no two have ever been the same, we have confirmed our belief in "nutritional individuality." This is not a new concept. Somewhere between 75 B.C. and 55 B.C., Lucretius wrote, "What is food to one man may be fierce poison to others."

To illustrate the significance of this new medical breakthrough, Cytotoxic testing, here is one of many case histories.

At sixty-nine years of age, one of Pat's favorite pastimes was ballroom dancing. For income, she took care of two elderly boarders at her home. She played the role of companion, as well as cook, housekeeper, and nurse. Walking up and down the stairs of her two-story home dozens of times each day, along with her nightly dancing routines, kept her in good shape.

A bout with the flu seemed to take the starch out of Pat, and, for some reason, instead of recovering, her symptoms worsened as time wore on. Doctors diagnosed and rediagnosed her condition. One thought she had arthritis, since she complained constantly of aching joints and muscles. Another thought she was imagining it all. She was never free of flulike symptoms, the worst of which were excruciating, debilitating headaches.

Over a period of six years, Pat was placed in the hospital, confined to bed, given drugs. One day a new doctor noticed a rash on her arms that was quite severe. A biopsy revealed lupus erythematosus, an acute and chronic skin disease of unknown origin. Certain cases can involve internal organs and can be fatal.

Treatment for lupus is uncertain, but to help relieve Pat's symptoms, the doctor prescribed 80 milligrams of cortisone every other day. She went into shock once, when she tried to quit taking it.

By this time, sapped of her strength, Pat got around only with the aid of a metal walker. She was never without pain and began drinking quantities of alcohol, explaining that it was the only way she could sleep at night. Pat ate "good food," a standard American diet of bacon and eggs for breakfast, and lots of beef and chicken.

Information on the Cytotoxic test came her way via a magazine article. She called long distance from Spokane and we arranged to have her blood sample drawn locally and shipped to our Los Angeles laboratory for the Cytotoxic analysis.

Her test showed nineteen reactions, chief among them the grains that go into alcohol, beef, sugar, yeast, and eggs. She avoided these substances completely, checking ingredients on every food package. For three days she suffered horrible headaches—withdrawal symptoms that will be discussed in later chapters. By the end of the fourth day she made a marked improvement. After sticking diligently to her diet for about two weeks, Pat showed a significant improvement. The pain began to subside and by the third week she no longer needed her walker.

When we last spoke, she was looking forward to resuming her dancing. She reported that her doctor was "shocked" at her sudden and total remission. He had reduced her cortisone intake to 10 milligrams. Soon she would be off the drug comppletely.

Strangely, while her doctor asked for copies of her diet and was adamant that she stick to it, my efforts to contact him for feedback were unsuccessful. I guess I don't blame him for hesitating. To many doctors, nutritional approaches to disease are threatening—even though many notable physicians, the famed Linus Pauling among them, are increasingly validating the importance of this approach. Eighty percent of my clients are medical doctors who have managed to bridge this gap. They have been astounded at the progress of many of their most difficult cases.

One case that particularly delighted me was Cathy, who when I met her was a bright, pretty thirteen-year-old who had lost all her hair. This sad sight at first made me think she'd been through chemotherapy or radiation treatments for cancer, which often leaves patients in this condition. But the source of Cathy's hair loss was a mystery. For several years, Cathy had seen an endless string of doctors and psychiatrists. Not one of them was able to give her any relief.

The Cytotoxic test came to her parents' attention through a magazine article; frankly, I believe they tried it as a last resort. They seemed to sense that the professionals they'd seen were barking up the wrong trees with their daughter and that somewhere, somehow, there would be an answer to Cathy's problem.

We performed the Cytotoxic test for Cathy, and it showed sensitivities to oranges and several other foods. When I talked to her after her test results were in, she told me she loved oranges. She craved them so much, in fact, that she always carried two or three with her to snack on. The test showed that Cathy had a severe reaction to oranges. She agreed to stop eating oranges and the other foods that showed white blood cell death during her test. New hair follicles soon began appearing.

There are thousands of other cases that make me feel just as gratified: ulcer patients can again enjoy food without suffering;

children, diagnosed as hyperactive, who are finally able to relax; or people who regain their sense of smell after suffering sinus congestion for years. And, of course, those who suffer so much in our society, people who are overweight—the dieters, who, after years of frustration, can achieve their appropriate body weight, painlessly, with an eating plan created distinctly for them by their own bodies.

My feeling about the Cytotoxic test is that it gives us away to understand what our bodies are trying to tell us. We Cytotoxic specialists feel we are standing on the threshold of a new era in health care, and we look to the future with an intense feeling of anticipation. We have discovered that the body's immune system—with its soldiers, the white blood cells—lies at the core of our deepest medical questions.

This book is a revealing beginning. Before we can reach our future goals, though, we must understand that we are each nutritionally unique. Our individual body blueprints map out our strengths and weaknesses, and we must attempt to discover how this uniqueness can work for us, making us the best we can be.

DOUG A. KAUFMANN

PART I

THE CYTOTOXIC EFFECT

A SCIENTIFIC APPROACH TO NUTRITION

1

The Cytotoxic Effect

This book is for people who are interested in building their endurance, increasing their mental and physical performance, correcting nutritional imbalances that cause disease, and maximizing their feeling of health and well-being.

When the body reacts in a negative way, whether it be simple skin rashes, painful chronic symptoms, or degenerative diseases, it's because there is breakdown in the immune system. The advent of the Cytotoxic test provides the first tangible evidence of a phenomenon that growing numbers of doctors have recently recognized and labeled "food sensitivity," the concept that certain food substances are toxic to the systems of certain people.

The Cytotoxic test is performed on a small blood sample drawn from a patient's arm. The sample is injected with tiny amounts of 180 or more different food substances. In the laboratory, a trained technician looks through a microscope and observes some of these food substances killing white blood cells, also called leukocytes, in the blood sample. No two people ever show the exact same set of sensitivities. What we all have in common, though, is that every one of us has *some* food sensitivities. And more often than not, the very foods we love and crave turn out to be toxic to our systems. We become addicted to these toxic foods, in much the same way that we get "hooked" on drugs, cigarettes, and alcohol.

What's the significance of the leukocyte death we observe under the microscope? Our white blood cells are the soldiers of our immune systems. They enable the body to fight infections and disease. What we see in the Cytotoxic test is a direct assault on the immune system by the foods we eat. We see the immune system being undermined, weakened. How can it protect us against serious disease, when the very foods we are eating every day keep it in a weakened state?

The Cytotoxic test shows that not only does this invisible enemy of health really exist but that each and every one of us has our own set of food sensitivities. Even those of us who feel healthy; even our children; yes, even the most "careful" eaters have toxic reactions to certain foods. These foods, when ingested, apparently play havoc with our immune systems and, over the long haul, weaken our defenses against serious disease. In case after case, we have found that when the offending substances are ferreted out and eliminated from the diet, the toxic reaction stops. Often diseases, some as serious as multiple sclerosis, Lupus, and arthritis, will go into remission. Other times, patients experience renewed strength and are able to fight back, at least keeping their illnesses contained. By eliminating foods to which we are reacting negatively, we free our immune system to do the job it was intended to do—protecting us from illness.

BACKGROUND: THE QUESTIONS THAT DEMANDED ANSWERS

Research on the Cytotoxic effect originated with Dr. William T. K. Bryan and Marian P. Bryan, researchers at the Washington University School of Medicine in St. Louis, who studied what they called the Cytotoxic Allergy Test. The term "Cytotoxic" is derived from "cyto," meaning cell, and "toxic," meaning poison. They performed the test on thousands of subjects, taking blood samples and injecting the samples with various food substances. Their findings showed that white blood cells underwent destruction as a result of the ingestion of certain foods by certain people. No two people would ever have the same reactions.

I studied with the Bryans in 1972 and subsequently returned to California and opened a research and testing laboratory. Working with biochemist Dr. Geoffrey Cheung, it soon became apparent that what we were witnessing in the Cytotoxic test's leukocyte death was actually the end of a long chain of biochemical events that led to the actual self-sacrificing of the white blood cells while trying to eliminate substances identified to them as foreign. This chain of events, we deduced, could explain the linking of nutritional deficiencies with all kinds of illness, both mental and physical.

In conventional medical circles, the linking of nutrition and disease is a recent phenomenon. While traditional folk medicine, many Eastern philosophies, and the profession of chiropractic all take foods into consideration when approaching healing, it was only in the early seventies that some American medical doctors began exploring the food/illness syndrome.

Their efforts began with a few medical heretics, like Linus Pauling, Ph.D., and Roger Williams, M.D. Pauling, the two-time Nobel Prize winner who coined the phrase "orthomolecular medicine" (treating diseases by varying the concentration of vitamins, minerals, trace elements, amino acids, enzymes, hormones, etc., in the body, laid the groundwork for others to rethink the medical establishment's long-held resistance to nutritional medicine. The scientific evidence and documented case histories that evolved through the work of these pioneers were hard to ignore, and increasing numbers of medical professionals began implementing these theories in their own work.

The subject of food allergy suddenly became a best-selling idea in the late seventies, when Dr. Marshall Mandell and Lynne Waller Scanlon wrote the book, *Dr. Mandell's Five Day*

Allergy Relief System, which he dedicated to the "countless millions of 'forgotten people' who are afflicted with diseases whose causes can be discovered and properly treated for the first time . . ."

A few years earlier, Dr. Claude Frazier had written *Coping with Food Allergy.* By 1980, the existence of the food allergy was fairly well accepted in traditional medical circles, and Theron Randolph, M.D., along with Dr. Ralph W. Moss gained national prominence with their book, *An Alternative Approach to Allergies.* The inevitable connection between food allergies and mental problems was finally made public by William H. Philpott, M.D., and Dr. Dwight K. Kalita in their book, *Brain Allergies, the Psychonutrient Connection.*

These books all dealt with the toxic effect of certain foods and nutritional deficiencies and their relation to diseases. The research centered around discovering what foods were toxic by putting the patient on a series of fasts and rotation diets. Even though the doctors' findings conflicted terribly with many of medicine's most cherished beliefs, their work gave thousands of patients relief from debilitating and previously unrelievable symptoms. It also provided clear scientific documentation for the existence of food sensitivities.

What was missing was a way to pinpoint the patient's food sensitivities quickly and easily; a method to take the guesswork and blind groping out of existing food sensitivity therapy. Something was needed, also, that would prove, in a clinical situation, that a toxic reaction was indeed taking place.

The Cytotoxic test provided this advance. After performing more than twenty thousand Cytotoxic tests in my laboratories, I can see that certain foods, like wheat and milk, affect the majority of us. The test has also shown that not one person has ever been tested 100 percent free of reactions.

SENSITIVITY, NOT ALLERGY

The Cytotoxic test is not an allergy test. Medical texts are correct in asserting that only about 3 to 7 percent of all people, at the very most, have food allergies. In fact, food allergies occurring after childhood are extremely rare. In general, if we have a food allergy, we know about it: the reaction is immediate and usually quite violent.

Most allergies are of the inhalant variety. The allergy is most commonly evidenced by a runny nose, watery eyes, itchiness, and skin eruptions like hives or rashes. These symptoms occur immediately following exposure to the offending substance, such as pollen or beestings. In some cases, certain foods, like milk products in a very few people, might bring about this Type I allergic reaction. Medically speaking, an allergy is a diverse immunological reaction to a substance that is harmless in similar amounts to other people. The immune system is involved to the extent that antibodies are secreted. If a substance, like strawberries, were to enter the body and elicit a secretion of any one of the antibodies, a whole chain of events would be triggered. The antibody circulates freely in the system, or it can bind with white blood cells. When the cell-bound antibody meets up with the antigen (the harmful substance, in this case strawberries), it initiates the allergic reaction within seconds. The white blood cells, once attacked by the antigen, explode and release histamines and other substances, and this leads to the symptom.

When a person faints from a beesting, develops hives from strawberries, or gets a runny nose from pollen spores in the air, he or she is experiencing a Type I, immediate hypersensitive reaction.

Another very dramatic allergic-type reaction is medically known as the food intolerance. Also rare, maybe 3 percent of the world's population suffer from intolerances. Those who do, though, are well aware of what they are. A food intolerance means that a given food cannot be assimilated or digested by the individual because the specific enzyme needed for the breakdown of that food is absent in that person's genetic makeup.

A common example of a food intolerance would be the lactase deficiency. A person who doesn't have the enzyme lactase cannot digest lactose, which is found in milk. While we have been conditioned to believe that milk is one of the "healthiest" foods we can eat, the truth is that part of the world's population is born without the lactase enzyme. These people can experience mild to heavy diarrhea, vomiting, sometimes even uncontrollable spasms just by drinking a glass of milk. Fortunately, in most of the cultures where lactase deficiency is common, cow's milk is not part of the diet.

The Cytotoxic test does not read allergies or intolerances. What it shows is another phenomenon altogether, one that is enthusiastically being called the major medical breakthrough of the eighties—food sensitivities.

Food sensitive reactions are technically called "delayed, masked, occult, hypersensitive reactions." What this lengthy name describes is a reaction that is not immediate, like the Type I allergic reaction, or the slightly delayed food intolerance reaction. Indeed, the carrot eaten on Sunday may show up as a headache on Tuesday. And if the sensitivity is abused over a number of years, it may, researchers are finding, very well turn up as a debilitating disease later on in life.

This delay in evident reaction is the chief reason food sensitivities have been such a long time in the discovery process. The headache victim rarely relates his affliction to the carrot he ate a day earlier. In fact, he would probably laugh if you told him that a carrot caused his headache. Likewise, we are not conditioned to equate our aching joints, breathing difficulties, lack of energy, and a propensity for "flu bugs" with the foods we eat. But we should! While these symptoms may be compounded by other physical or emotional factors, the food sensitivity is often at the root of the problem. The following chart, taken from *Tracking Down Hidden Food Allergies* by William G. Crook, M.D., shows what connections we can make.

Common Symptoms of Food Sensitivities

Physical Symptoms

Head	Headaches, fainting, dizziness, feeling of fullness in the head, excessive drowsiness or sleepiness soon after eating, insomnia
Eyes, ears, nose, and throat	Runny nose, stuffy nose, excessive mucus formation, watery eyes, blur-

ring of vision, ringing in the ears, earache, fullness in the ears, fluid in the middle ear, hearing loss, recurrent ear infections, itching ear, ear drainage, sore throats, chronic cough, gagging, canker sores, itching of the roof of the mouth, recurrent sinusitis

Heart and lungs	Palpitations, increased heart rate, rapid heart rate (tachycardia) asthma, congestion in the chest, hoarseness
Gastrointestinal	Nausea, vomiting, diarrhea, constipation, bloating after meals, belching, colitis, flatulence, feeling of fullness in the stomach long after finishing a meal, abdominal pains or cramps
Skin	Hives, rashes, eczema, dermatitis, pallor
Other symptoms	Chronic fatigue; weakness; muscle aches and pains; joint aches and pains; swelling of the hands, feet, or ankles; urinary tract symptoms (frequency, urgency); vaginal discharge; hunger (and its close ally, binge or spree eating)

Psychological
Symptoms

Anxiety, panic attacks, depression, crying jags, aggressive behavior, irritability, mental dullness, mental lethargy, confusion, excessive daydreaming, hyperactivity, restlessness, learning disabilities, poor work habits, slurred speech, stuttering, inability to concentrate, indifference

2

Nutritional Individuality

There are new plateaus to reach in living healthy lives. I doubt seriously that there are many of us who realize just how healthy we can be; how easily and brilliantly our minds and bodies are meant to function. Emerging from the syndromes that keep us weakened and ill is possible, but it means reevaluating the way we observe ourselves.

First of all, let's forget about everything we've ever heard or read about nutrition.

Now, we'll gather up all the fad diet books and "good food" cookbooks we've been collecting and pile them up in a corner.

We are about to break away from the masses to whom these systems cater and realize that what we are, what we were always meant to be is, in a word, *unique.*

The missing link in our approach to combating illness is quite simply, our individuality. Each person has a human blueprint. We each have a unique set of genetic information in each of our 200 billion cells; we each look different; we each have different fingerprints and dental charts. How can we possibly approach our physical problems by being so general? Of the many approaches to health, to dieting, to keeping fit, not one of them really can work for all of us.

Medical approaches stressing individual needs were first brought to public attention in 1965 by Dr. Roger J. Williams, who coined the phrase "biochemical individuality." During the years that followed, many others in the medical profession followed his lead, trying to discover each person's biochemical uniqueness. I feel that in this discovery lies the key to health.

Of the more than twenty thousand Cytotoxic tests my laboratories have processed, no two have ever had the same results. Parents and children, brothers and sisters, people who grow up in similar climates or who have the same diet or eating habits—they share some sensitivities, but no two sets of food sensitivities are completely alike. This is nutritional individuality. And its discovery must alter the way we have been dealing with our lives.

Nutritional individuality also shows us that we need to explore further the way we approach major issues affecting our culture. In my opinion, the alcohol rehabilitation program, for example, that ignores grain sensitivity cannot effectively rehabilitate an alcoholic. Doctors are treating symptoms, not touching the roots of the problem. Many alcoholics now know they are dealing with an allergy to alcohol. In fact, alcohol rehabilitation programs have adopted this theory as part of their postulates on alcohol addiction. What they have yet to realize, though, is that they are dealing with more than an allergic reaction to alcohol: the grains from which the alcohol is made apparently lie at the core of the problem.

Taking nutritional individuality into consideration would also drastically change the way we treat children who have learning disabilities or who have trouble paying attention in the classroom. Sometimes we isolate them; often we frustrate ourselves trying to invent teaching aids that will arouse their interest. We should test them for toxic substances that are, without a doubt, in their systems. The child may have nothing

more than a sensitivity to the milk he is drinking or the bread
he is eating during "nutrition" period. Astounding as this may
sound, there are now substantial numbers of documented case
histories proving the relationship of food sensitivity to learning
disorders.

Whole wheat bread, whose virtues are extolled in health and
diet books, is actually a killer of white blood cells in many thousands, maybe millions of people. In fact, next to milk, wheat is
the most common source of food sensitivity. Dr. Harsha V. Dehigia, president of the Allergy Information Association, writes
in *The Allergy Book, a Family Guide* that wheat allergies and
intolerances are common. He reports that wheat often causes
newborn babies to develop rashes, colic, and diarrhea when
first introduced to cereal in their diet. It may also cause older
children to exhibit eczema or asthma. Treating schizophrenia
by eliminating wheat products is well documented in Dr. William Philpott's book, *Brain Allergies.* In his book, *Eating and
Allergy,* Robert Eagle talks about wheat allergy and its effects
on the brain. He writes that doctors at the National Institute of
Mental Health Research have found that partially digested gluten (a substance found in wheat products) can act in the brain
in exactly the same way as opiate drugs.

This is not meant to negate the nutritional properties of
wheat or milk. They are healthful foods for many people. The
point is they are not good for *everyone.*

Our nutritional individuality is so obvious that one wonders
why it has been noticed in only the most superficial ways over
the years. One reason could be that it has never before been
possible to prove, scientifically, the link between food sensitivities and physical or mental ailments. The Cytotoxic test is providing this proof.

Much of our existing medical technology is based on norms
extrapolated from records and statistics. There seem to be few,
if any, norms to be found when analyzing the returns from Cytotoxic testing. This confounds many members of the medical
establishment, a profession accustomed to using these norms
for many of its procedures and diagnoses. One example, not as
widespread as it once was but still quite prevalent, is the routine and unnecessary removal of tonsils in children.

We also impose norms on ourselves. Think of the countless numbers of suffering people trying diet after diet to achieve what Madison Avenue has them believing are "normal" weight levels. Many people's bone structures call for a higher or lower than "normal" weight level.

Perhaps one of the most abusive norms we have created are the Recommended Dietary Allowances (RDAs), established decades ago by the Food and Nutrition Board of the National Academy of Sciences and used as a basis for the Food and Drug Administration's famous Minimum Daily Requirements (MDRs) of nutrients that we find listed on the back of cereal boxes and on bread wrappers. Most of us think that RDAs tell us how many units of each vitamin and mineral our bodies should have. Actually, they list only a small number of essential nutrients at a level approximated to be required by the human body only to avoid serious illness. The .45 milligrams of ascorbic acid (vitamin C), for example, that we find listed in the MDRs is sufficient only to alleviate and cure the clinical signs of scurvy. According to the National Academy of Sciences' own book, *Recommended Dietary Allowances:* "This amount, however, may not be satisfactory for the maintenance of optimal health over long periods of time." The NAS stresses that "the requirement for a nutrient is the minimum intake that will maintain normal function and health," not the amount of the nutrient that will create a state of optimal health, as we are led to believe. This, they say in no uncertain terms, differs among individuals and from time to time for a given individual whose needs change with stress, climate, and other factors. They are, without realizing it, confirming the existence of nutritional individuality.

Yet, while the NAS, a United States government agency, itself declares the inadequacy of its RDAs, we all use them as a guide when reading vitamin bottle labels, choosing breakfast cereals, and making other important nutritional choices. In fact, it's something we rarely question.

While many branches of medicine depend on norms to a great extent, there is one kind of doctor, the orthomolecular physician, who especially stresses individuality in his treatment of illness. The field of orthomolecular medicine was started in

1968 by Nobel Prize winner Dr. Linus Pauling as an approach to healing that treats disease and infection by varying the concentrations of vitamins, minerals, and other nutritional substances that are normally present in the body. Orthomolecular physicians believe that healthy cells make for healthy bodies and healthy minds. They use nutrients instead of drugs, whenever possible, to treat illness. Their results can only be described as startling and monumental.

The cornerstone of orthomolecular medicine is biochemical and nutritional individuality, for it is only in the discovery of each patient's cellular deficiencies and particular food sensitivities that the physician is able to correct the balance of nutrients in that person. It's no easy task to ferret out these weak points. It takes patience, trial and error, and then more patience. But time and time again, their efforts prove worthwhile.

The advent of the Cytotoxic test has provided orthomolecular medicine with a fast and relatively inexpensive means of discovering the individual substances that are toxic to patients. At least one phase of their investigation has been made easy. According to Harvey Ross, M.D., president of the Academy of Orthomolecular Psychiatry, "Determining food allergies and sensitivities is frequently a most crucial aspect of our work. Whether we're dealing with extreme cases of schizophrenia or with people who are functioning in the world but who still suffer from depressions, hypoglycemia, or an inability to handle stress, we have found that allergies and sensitivities often play a significant part in causing symptoms."

Prior to Cytotoxic testing, the only methods used to discover toxic reactions from food were at best unsatisfactory, says Dr. Ross. There were sublingual tests, where suspected allergens are placed under the tongue of the patient, who was then monitored for reactions. There were the common skin "scratch tests," where the suspected allergen is placed under the patient's skin, and again, monitoring takes place. These tests are expensive, sometimes painful, extremely time consuming, and, in rare instances, they can trigger severe allergic reaction.

More recently, RAST (Radio Allergo Sorbent Test) was developed, which is performed on a sample of the patient's blood. Although, again, this test is limited and expensive, it is the best method available to isolate inhalant or airborne allergies. The main objection to all these tests, say physicians trying to discover their patients' food toxicities, is that they give readings on Type I allergic reactions only. They do not read food sensitivities.

A method for discovering food sensitivities was set forth by a famous allergist, Theron Randolph, M.D., who developed a regimen that involves a four-day fast and then one-at-a-time food challenges with the patient being monitored for reactions. Needless to say, the patient must be hospitalized for this test. Also, while the average Cytotoxic test includes about two hundred foods, it would not be possible to test a patient for this many substances using Dr. Randolph's methods.

The Cytotoxic test gives doctors the tool they have been looking for—a simple, accurate, inexpensive way to start their investigation. Now that the Cytotoxic test has been widely used and its results documented, we find that there are ways for people to isolate some of their major sensitivities without taking the test. The first step is simply to eliminate from your diet those foods you crave or those foods you find yourself eating most regularly. Carefully review and utilize the charts in Chapter 9. Be honest in your assessment, though, because you have only yourself to fool.

During this elimination period, you may feel unbearable cravings for a few days; these are withdrawal reactions. After the first four days, you will probably experience a few weeks of supersensitivity to the food substances you have eliminated, so read labels on packaged foods carefully to make sure you don't accidentally slip the food into your diet. Eliminate the food, or foods, entirely for a few months, if you can. Be assured, you will feel the difference mentally and physically in many, many ways.

3

Optimizing Health by Listening to Your Body

"But doctor, I've tried everything . . . ! "

Health is a very positive word. We aren't healthy simply because we don't feel sick; we are healthy because all of our body functions are properly tuned, making us feel absolutely great. Yet most of us think of health only as an absence of symptoms.

What is a healthy body? It's one that doesn't fight itself. The healthy body is neither too fat nor too thin, its weight is appropriate to its genetic makeup and bone structure. A healthy body is comfortable in most surroundings. It is energetic and recuperates quickly when caught by "flu bugs" and viral infections. Most of the time it doesn't get "caught" at all.

The healthy body rests well during sleep and awakens refreshed and energized, giving the mind a feeling of peace and well-being. Remember, your body and mind are linked together. While a healthy body may ache when not exercised properly, it reacts quickly, even joyfully, and swiftly tones itself when given attention.

Optimizing your health means achieving the greatest state of health possible, considering your environment and genetic makeup. I know very few people who can honestly say they experience a state of optimum health. Many of us strive for it, but few ever achieve it. We *could* have it, but instead opt to spend our days actively ignoring the messages our bodies send out, messages telling us that things are not working perfectly. Through this avoidance, we allow serious illness to develop.

Obviously, there are real constraints that keep us in a substandard state of health. Our food is contaminated with many toxic substances we don't know about. So is the air we breathe. Even noncontaminated foods may, as we show in this book, cause all kinds of physical and mental weaknesses. We spend most of our waking hours in work situations that don't allow for proper exercise. But even *with* these constraints, most of us can achieve a state of health far superior to what we now experience. First we must learn to listen to our bodies and to understand that the various aches, discomforts, stuffy noses, fatigue, digestive problems, and all the rest are silent but clear signals that changes need to be made.

We all suffer from discomforts, yet we remain casual about them, dismissing them in various ways. Often I'll hear a person say of his chronic depression, "It's just the way I am." Another will assure me that his constantly aching joints "run in the family." Ringing in the ears is something "I'll just have to learn to live with."

When we tire of these excuses, we quickly find others for our itchy eyes, stomach cramps, and headaches. The weather has been a "cause" of many an inexplicable symptom, probably since man first began to communicate. Today we have a more trendy, but equally pervasive bad guy: stress syndrome.

The pimply faced teenager will often blame his affliction on his genetic makeup. But those who once blamed chocolate for acne breakouts were probably closer to the truth. Now we can take it a step farther and add perhaps dairy products, wheat, eggs, or even beans or carrots.

We devote vast amounts of time and energy to discomfort avoidance. If you doubt this, just take a look at the thousands of over-the-counter medications that are sold to alleviate our everyday symptoms. We are frightened by these symptoms and will often do anything we can to make them disappear.

Many of us operate at an extremely low threshold of tolerance to stress, both physical and mental. A harsh word from a friend or sometimes even a newspaper story is enough to send some people into a thorough depression. Many of us find ourselves catching one cold or virus after another. And all the vitamins in the world don't seem to help. In most cases, this lowered threshold is a result of the weakening of the body's immune system by food sensitivities, because toxic foods add yet more stress to the existing load.

SENSITIVITY THRESHOLDS

One of the difficulties in isolating and connecting a food sensitivity to a particular symptom is that the symptoms often vary in intensity. Some of them don't noticeably appear every time the offending food is eaten. There is sometimes a delay from the time the food is eaten to the time the symptom appears. In extreme instances, this lapse can be as much as four or five days. That's why a food sensitivity is known as a delayed, masked, occult hypersensitivity. These variations result from the constant changing of each individual's sensitivity threshold.

Every one of us can tolerate a certain amount of allergens or toxic substances entering our bodies, either through the foods we eat, the air we breathe, or the chemicals that come in contact with our skin. The point at which the immune system becomes overloaded and a symptom appears is called the sensitivity threshold. Once this threshold is crossed, the immune system breaks down, and the body can no longer tolerate additional toxic insult.

I often have people tell me that after they eliminate for a few months all the substances that showed up as toxic on their Cytotoxic tests, they are able to reintroduce certain reactive foods without a problem. What they are experiencing is a heightening of their sensitivity thresholds, enabling their bodies to tolerate quantities of substances that would in the past have caused a reaction. For instance, though I am sensitive to wheat, I can eat a sandwich once a week or so without having a significant reaction to the bread.

Stresses of various kinds can make our sensitivity thresholds swing like pendulums. When we constantly assault our immune systems with toxic foods, we are creating stress. Couple this with the day-to-day emotional, mental, and physical stresses we all encounter; add to that an additional stress, like a seasonal pollen allergy, and you can find yourself in a state of chronic hypersensitization. Your sensitivity threshold becomes so low that your body can hardly tolerate a thing. Enter an infection, like a virus, and you may suddenly become seriously ill.

In his book, *The Stress of Life,* Dr. Hans Selye describes three stages of stress: alarm, adaptation, and exhaustion.

In the alarm phase, we first encounter something foreign or dangerous to our lives. The body reacts by releasing hormones, like adrenaline, to deal with the situation. During the adaptation phase, the body will try to adapt itself to the stress, in order to continue living. When the stress combines with other stresses or overwhelms the body's ability to adapt to it, the third phase, exhaustion, sets in. At this point, the threshold is lowered and the foods to which we are sensitive become powerful symptom producers. The cycle is a vicious one, for once the threshold is lowered, the body is unable to cope with infections that cross its path. These, once established, keep the threshold lowered.

An example is Molly, who became ill at the very point in her life when she should have been the happiest, on her honeymoon. Molly was enjoying the tropical sun and foods at a resort hotel on Maui, one of the Hawaiian Islands.

But a helicopter ride to a more remote island, Kaui, changed things and actually became a turning point in her life. During the short trip, the new bride felt slightly nauseated and dizzy, but it was nothing she took very seriously until her symptoms failed to subside—not the next day or the next week or even after she got home.

While in Hawaii, she found many things to blame for her general malaise: the hot humid air, the lack of air conditioning in her room, the new kinds of foods she was eating. As the days wore on, though, these excuses began to run thin, and the nausea was now accompanied by strong stomach cramps, severe constipation, and splitting headaches.

Molly assumed she'd picked up some kind of tropical virus. She had been prone to constipation from time to time since childhood, and occasional headaches were certainly no stranger to her. But suddenly it seemed as if all these problems were piling on at once.

After her honeymoon, Molly took her illness home with her. She felt sleepy and nauseated all the time and sought relief through a doctor. She began a series of tests. An upper GI series (X rays of the upper gastrointestinal tract, often used to check for ulcers) showed nothing. Neither did a chest X ray or an entire battery of blood tests. A five-hour glucose tolerance test advised by her internist showed, during the fourth hour, a severe drop in blood sugar level, and Molly was diagnosed as hypoglycemic and put on a high-protein/sugar-free diet. The diet gave her some relief from the tiredness she had been feeling, but she was still nauseated twenty-four hours a day. She couldn't explain the general lack of energy and depression she felt.

Frustrated, the young woman was about to return to Hawaii, thinking that perhaps she was suffering from some kind of "island fever" that an island doctor might recognize. Just as she was about to make a decision, a friend told her about food sensitivities and the Cytotoxic test. It made sense to her, since the only glimmer of relief she'd been able to achieve was from her hypoglycemic diet. Maybe foods *were* involved in the rest of her symptoms as well. She took a Cytotoxic test in September 1981 and had thirty-two reactions, about average. Many of them were the common sensitivities a majority of us share: coffee, oats, rye, chocolate, shrimp.

But the one that I feel made Molly cross her allergic threshold while on her honeymoon in Hawaii was a food that showed a strong Cytotoxic reaction on her test—pineapple. Anyone who has been to Hawaii knows that the island pineapples are a treat to the senses. Sweet, flavorful, juicy, and freshly picked, the pineapples are included with almost every Hawaiian meal. Molly was no exception. She loved them, but they hated her!

Once her allergic threshold was crossed by overdosing on

pineapples, Molly's symptoms flared up. While she was sensitive to a great many of her favorite foods, they seemingly did not place too much of an allergic load on her until the pineapple. In Hawaii, the poor girl started reacting to everything. The helicopter ride added just enough stress to undermine her immune system. We often see this happen. It was only after Molly isolated and eliminated thirty-two intolerant foods that she was able to build up her immune system again and get rid of the other symptoms she was feeling.

She now reports that there are certain foods she reacts to immediately, but most of the foods that showed up as sensitive on her Cytotoxic test have been successfully reintroduced into her diet. As long as she keeps rotating them, not repeating a single food more than once every four days (see Chapter 10), she feels fine. The period of total elimination she required was about two months.

LISTENING TO YOUR BODY

People come in to take a Cytotoxic test hoping to cure their migraine headaches and often end up telling me that not only did their headaches disappear but they suddenly found that they were losing weight and feeling more able to cope with their relationships—job changes—even life-styles.

By ignoring our symptoms, we allow them to grow into illnesses and permanent injuries to our organs, nerves, and tissues. If we learn to listen to our bodies, we can halt the progress of this chain of events before it's too late. There is an inborn ability—we all have it—to communicate with our bodies. It isn't difficult. We just don't develop this capacity in our culture, but it's worth cultivating.

The process requires only some quiet time, say ten minutes, each day. Try it now, as you read this chapter. Turn your thoughts inward and begin with the obvious. Are you experiencing a bloated, gassy feeling? Is there perhaps a mild headache or maybe a stuffy nose? Is your throat tight or a little sore? Think carefully. We tend to become jaded to these symptoms, accepting them as normal, and you may not notice them at first.

When you first sat down to read, was it painful to bend? Was it difficult to focus your eyes on the printed page? Do you feel your attention drifting?

If you experience any of these symptoms, your body is probably telling you that something isn't working quite right. If we can catch these signals while they are still "whispering" their needs, we can avoid illness trends that are difficult and sometimes impossible to turn around. The best way to monitor the body for signals is to do something I refer to as "body scanning." This exercise is a tremendous relaxation technique as well as a way to put your mind and body together for a while.

Prior to going to sleep tonight, take a few minutes, lie flat on your back, and let your mind clear itself of everyday thoughts. Close your eyes and guide your senses to your inner being.

To begin, mentally focus on you toes. Slowly bend each one, monitoring for any hint of pain or cramping. Bend the ankles and then flex the calf muscles. Use your hands. Are there tender spots? Is there pain when you flex and then relax the muscles? Feel the skin surface. It should be smooth, cool to the touch. Are there rashes, itchy spots? Is the area around the kneecap tender? Are the thigh muscles relaxed? Let your hands follow your mental journey up your body. If the muscles feel locked and tired, or the skin is sensitive to the touch, your body could be signaling a need for exercise and toning. It could also be expressing symptoms of toxic reactions to the foods you have been eating. Always keep in mind while reading this book that symptoms, no matter how slight, may be signaling a more serious condition, like an organ malfunction, or even tumor growth.

As you use all your inner senses to scan your body, think about the feelings you are experiencing. Are you feeling anxious? Restless? Or are you confident and relaxed? If you are at all apprehensive, it's possible that you have been avoiding some of these signals, even without realizing it.

What colors come to mind as your focus your attention on your inner body? Do you picture bright, pink, healthy colors? Or are you shadowed by gray, dingy tones? Picture your organs—the liver, kidneys, intestines. Are they running smoothly?

If you allow them to, your kinesthetic senses will speak to you in pictures, colors, images, and feelings. Developing these senses will lead to a lifetime of increased health. Any medical doctor will tell you that a patient who is able to get in touch with his body has the greatest chance of a speedy and full recovery from even the most serious illness. The person who can tap into the body's vast communications network is the one who will understand what is going on inside and who can apply his mind and body to the recovery process. With practice, the pictures and images we get can become incredibly clear.

With this awareness as you go through your normal day-to-day routine, try to notice other possible body signals. Do you suffer from facial twitches when under stress? Do you experience mood swings at certain times each day? Do you feel lightheaded after lunch?

Some body signals occur only when certain stresses and toxic food reactions combine. So be aware of your body throughout your day. Try to remember what you have eaten just before the onset of a headache, or exactly what you had for lunch when you experience the afternoon "sleepies." Concentrate on your repetitive eating habits.

We react to the foods our body is sensitive to in many ways. As I mentioned earlier in the chapter, rarely do people exhibit only one symptom. They may have one major complaint, but are multisymptomatic. These symptom combinations often "snowball" over time. The mild headache we experienced occasionally after lunch in high school becomes an everyday occurrence in college. As years pass, the headache grows in intensity, until it is accompanied by a feeling of nausea. The problem, if not identified (and drug therapy doesn't identify problems), grows and speaks louder and louder until, one day, we are forced to listen. By then it's sometimes too late.

FOOD SENSITIVITIES AND SYMPTOMS

One question I am asked over and over again is how does the apple to which a person is sensitive translate into a headache or hurting joint? How do the wheat or dairy products so many of us show sensitivities to cause stuffy noses? Depressions? Why do different foods produce different reactions in different people? If you and I are both sensitive to peaches, why would they give you a headache and me a skin rash?

Dr. Geoffrey Cheung, a biochemist and one of the leading researchers in the field of Cytotoxic testing, has broken new ground with his explanations of the linking between food sensitivities and various symptoms.

At the core of Dr. Cheung's thinking is the phenomenon of edema, or tissue swelling, caused by cells in various parts of the body retaining water in response to an influx of toxic foods. When the body takes in a substance it identifies as foreign or toxic, the cells will attempt to detoxify themselves by taking on water, trying to dilute the toxins. Rob Krakovitz, M.D., who uses the Cytotoxic test extensively in his holistic medical practice, explains, "The body has a certain wisdom that I've come to trust. I think the cells know about self-preservation." The cells know that their chances for survival are better if they can dilute the toxin. Even biologically simple organisms like jellyfish or corals will take on water to detoxify themselves. This cellular wisdom sets the stage for a symptom to appear—a signal that help is needed.

When a cell takes on water, it expands and can put pressure on surrounding cells. If these neighboring cells happen to be nerve cells, pain or numbness or confusion will result.

Another consequence of cell expansion, or swelling, is the constriction of tiny capillaries in the area of the toxic assault. This restricts the flow of blood, which carries much needed oxygen to the cells. When the flow is restricted, a lack of oxygen, or anoxia, results. At the far end of the restricted capillary, the wisdom of the cells once again comes into play. Because cells require oxygen in order to convert foodstuffs to energy, they will "cut their power," or decrease their activity when the oxygen supply is diminished. In order to decrease activity, the cell must let go of some of its underoxidized by-products, usually lactic acid. This acid, after leaving the cell, can attack surrounding nerve endings—another cause of painful symptoms.

An example of lactic acid release occurs when a runner experiences painful leg cramps. These are caused by a lactic acid buildup. The runner's leg muscles are burning oxygen much faster than his capillaries can supply fresh oxygen to the cells. So the cells spill out their lactic acid, which "pickles" the muscle and causes a cramp.

Another example of tissue swelling can be seen in the person with an allergy who can't smell his food. The allergic reaction causes his nasal tissue to swell around the olfactory nerve. This swelling constricts the nerve and keeps neural synapsis (the electronic/chemical transmission of messages from nerve to brain) from taking place. The olfactory nerve, which is responsible for the sense of smell, and therefore for taste pinch your nose when eating and you won't be able to taste your food), is unable to get the message to the brain, and the sense of smell is inhibited.

While some nasal conditions are the result of inhalant allergies, like pollen or dust or animal fur, many others are caused by food sensitivities. Don't be tricked into believing that all allergic-type sinus reactions are caused by airborne spores. Sometimes a combination of both food sensitivities and inhalant allergies exists, and eliminating toxic foods can still give immeasurable relief. A good way to judge which kind of reaction you are having is to ask yourself whether your nose is stuffy all year long, or if the stuffiness is only a seasonal or occasional thing. If it's seasonal or occasional, chances are pollen or other airborne particles are to blame. If it's a year-round, no-matter-where-you-are type of condition, food sensitivities must be considered.

Krakovitz says that whenever a patient comes into his office complaining of a postnasal drip that's been going on constantly for years, it's a clue that food sensitivities are at work. In one case, a seventy-three-year-old man who was active and in good general health came to him complaining of an arthritic condition he'd had for the preceding twenty-five years. He'd been taking popular arthritis drugs for almost twenty years to help relieve his symptoms. He also had a postnasal drip and suffered from indigestion. The man took a Cytotoxic test and turned out to be sensitive to wheat, among other things. He eliminated these substances, and his arthritis pain disappeared within two weeks. When some time went by, he decided to test some of these foods by reintroducing them, one at a time, into his diet. When he tested the wheat, his joint pain flared up. Without wheat, the symptom again disappeared in a week. To make sure he wasn't imagining things, he ate a large quantity of wheat. He suffered a severe and painful relapse that lasted for two weeks after he again stopped eating the substance. He can still reproduce his symptoms at any time by eating wheat. His postnasal drip now gives him trouble only rarely—something that could be due to an inhalant allergy.

The tissue swelling caused by eating foods that are toxic to the body may certainly be part of the arthritic condition. I feel, after working with hundreds of people with joint pain, that most types of arthritis are allergic or sensitivity reactions. The connection is too apparent to be ignored.

What makes a joint painful? Ingesting foods that are toxic to the body triggers the cellular water retention we have been discussing in this chapter. We see a swelling of the soft tissue in the joint or in the bursal linings of the bone itself. This puts pressure on the surrounding nerves, and pain and immobility result.

Why are some organs affected in a particular person and not in others? Dr. Krakovitz feels that genetics are involved. Weak genetic tendencies mean that certain organs will be the first to break down under stress. In one person it will be the digestive tract. In another the joints. And in still another, the cerebral tissues will feel the effects.

Genetic predisposition is not the only reason an organ or particular body system will produce symptoms. The unique stresses—emotional, physical, and chemical—that we each put on our bodies can cause the breakdown of specific body parts. The variables are endless, making it difficult to speculate where the sensitivity symptom will appear.

OVERWEIGHT: A TOXIC REACTION TO INCOMPATIBLE FOODS?

The stomach area is especially vulnerable to food sensitivities, since it's the seat of digestion (or lack thereof), one of the first places a toxic food might be felt. The problem of overweight is grossly misunderstood in medicine today. As long as toxic foods are eaten and the cells retain water in an attempt to detoxify themselves, enduring weight loss can never occur. That's why very few of the hundreds of diet books and weight loss programs appear to be useful in the long run.

Anyone who has ever tried in earnest to lose weight has probably noticed an immediate drop in weight during the first week or so of a diet. After this initial drop, the pounds come off much more slowly. We often hear people referring to this immediate weight loss as "only losing excess water." Isn't it curious that no one questions the cause of water retention? The answer clearly emerges when we examine the Cytotoxic effect. The ingestion of toxic substances causes the cells in the tissue surrounding the stomach, hips, thighs, or anywhere in the body to retain water.

Dr. Cheung's research has illuminated the biochemical process linking food sensitivity to overweight. At the root of the problem is the secretion of steroids. When toxins are ingested into the body, a physiological stress situation is produced. The body has certain ways of dealing with stress. In this case, the stress signal goes up and the pituitary gland sends hormones, or chemical messengers, to certain targets, like the adrenal glands. The adrenal glands receive the message and, in turn, secrete steroids. These steroids, most often cortisol and hydrocortisol are chemical agents sent by the adrenals to other organs, mainly the liver. The liver, upon recognizing the steroid, immediately changes its pattern of metabolism.

Normally, the liver metabolizes carbohydrates (grains, sugars) by turning them into sugars, then into energy, and then into the waste product, carbon dioxide, which is breathed out through the lungs. When the steroids deliver the message from the adrenals, the liver changes its pattern and begins to turn the carbohydrates into fatty acids instead of sugars. These fatty acids combine and form macrolipids, or large fat globules.

The removal of toxic foods from the system reverses the stress situation; thus, the secretion of steroids decreases. Occasionally, the hypersteroid condition will have gone too far and will not reverse. But this is the exception, not the rule.

Tissue edema in relation to overweight is a well-established medical fact. What's new, however, and what we see daily in

our Cytotoxic research, is the linking of the steroid secretion to
the ingestion of toxins, with flabbiness as the end result. That's
why cutting calories to lose weight is a losing proposition in every way but weight loss. When a patient isolates the foods to
which his body is sensitive and he avoids those foods and ro-
tates the others to keep from building new sensitivities (see
Chapters 9 and 10), he allows his cells to achieve a reasonable
degree of balance.

The same rule applies to the other symptoms we've been ad-
dressing in this chapter. By listening to your body, you may be
able to hear its signals while they are still fairly subtle. By far,
the best way to cure serious illness is to prevent it. Learning to
recognize the symptoms of toxic reactions is the best way to
avoid their building into disease spirals.

4

Cerebral
Food Sensitivities

The brain—its mysteries continue to elude our most sophisticated medical technology. We remain in awe of its power and are baffled by the magnitude of its abilities. Yet the brain is the most vulnerable organ in our bodies, lacking even an ability to defend itself against toxic attack, as our other organs do.

A mass of soft tissue made of billions of cells, experts say that at best we use about 10 percent of its creative, logical, and reactive capabilities. Why don't we use the rest? Why do so many millions of us have trouble even maintaining our 10 percent level? Why, with all our modern technology and powerful drugs, are our mental institutions bursting at the seams with people who, for one reason or another, are unable to function in the world?

Responding to minute, almost undetectable electronic and chemical impulses emanating from the body's entire nervous system, the brain regulates and rules every single move we make, every thought we think, every feeling we have. No wonder nature provided for the brain first when it created its superhighway, the circulatory system, wherein nutrients and valuable oxygen travel to their ultimate destinations. The very first branch of the aortic arch that carries fresh, nutrient- and oxygen-rich blood from the heart goes straight up to the brain.

By the same token, the brain is also the first to receive toxic substances. These toxins, often foods to which the body is sensitive or toxic chemicals that are inhaled, cause the brain to produce symptoms. It can retain water and swell, just like other body tissue, causing splitting headaches and a multitude of other symptoms. These symptoms are all too familiar to most of us.

What we must realize is that the brain, as wondrous as it is, is simply an organ of the body and is as susceptible as any other organ to toxic reactions. But instead of skin rashes, joint pains, or stuffy noses, brain sensitivities bring about depressions, fatigue, learning disorders, anxiety attacks, insomnia, hyperactivity, personality changes, emotional outbursts, schizophrenia, dizziness, headaches of all kinds, and a whole array of brain function disorders. The brain, like any other organ, is using these symptoms to signal that something is wrong, that something needs attention.

It's difficult to imagine the depths of mental anguish sometimes suffered by those with cerebral sensitivities until someone close to you is affected by them. You can only watch helplessly as that person goes from doctor to doctor, from psychiatrist to institution. As the symptoms intensify, so do the drugs prescribed to dull the feelings.

When we observe foods to which a person is sensitive killing his white blood cells during the Cytotoxic test, we are witnessing an attack on the person's immune system. How does a weakened immune system affect the brain?

Biochemist Dr. Geoffrey Cheung has spent years studying the Cytotoxic effect and its relation to cerebral malfunction. He explains that brain cells are highly specialized, each with its own defined function. Unlike cells in other parts of the body, cerebral cells are not readily able to adapt to substandard conditions. While other cells limit their function in order to survive a toxic attack (see preceding chapter), brain cells are incapable of much adaptation. Also, while other cells in the body have control over their membrane permeability and can keep many toxic substances from entering, brain cells have very little control over what gets in. This makes them extremely vulnerable. As if that weren't enough, the brain lacks certain cells found only in the circulatory system, commonly known as the B and T lymphocytes. The T lymphocytes carry the memory codes that recognize foreign matter and the B lymphocytes are involved with the secretion of the immunoglobulins based upon signals from the T cells. Between the B and T lymphocytes, foreign matter is recognized and the immune system is commanded to attack. Without B and T cells, the brain can do very little to alleviate its situation when foreign substances are present.

Cerebral immunological response is also very limited, and brain cells are equipped for defense only. There is no attack mechanism. What the brain can and does do is try to adjust to an invading army of toxins. And, by the way, these poisons can be broccoli or chocolate or hard drugs. They can be milk or wheat or hemlock—anything that is identified as foreign by the individual's system. This identification occurs as soon as a substance enters the mouth and comes in contact with the glands under the tongue.

The brain cells adjusts to this toxic assault by switching from normal foodstuff breakdown to short-term energy production. This massive influx of energy helps the brain cope with the toxic assault by shoring up the cell linings, thus keeping the cells' permeability to a minimum. When this happens, normal functions are interrupted, and you end up with a neural aberration. This occurs to everyone all the time, many times during each day. Needless to say, when it happens too much, we begin to notice symptoms. It is not difficult to imagine, therefore, how the brain can produce a feeling of listlessness, fatigue, despondency, or confusion in response to an avalanche of toxic assaults, or why it becomes so difficult to concentrate at times, or why there seems to be no energy to emerge from even a mild depression or bad mood.

Mental ailments are all too often called emotional "hang-ups." Sometimes, serious mental illnesses like schizophrenia are considered progressive diseases or even genetic tendencies. Now, through study of the Cytotoxic effect, these problems can often be linked to the foods we eat and their ravaging effects on our brains.

Awareness of the weakening of cerebral function by attacks of toxic substances is relatively new to the medical profession. But I believe, as do the many physicians and psychiatrists I work with, that the vast majority of people who are now institutionalized for various mental illnesses are, in actuality, suffering from a combination of food and chemical allergies and sensitivities.

The pioneering work of orthomolecular psychiatrist William H. Philpott in cases of severe psychotic and especially schizophrenic patients—people who did not respond to traditional drug or electroshock therapies—speaks for itself. Philpott, who wrote *Brain Allergies* in 1980 with Dr. Dwight Kalita, relies on what he calls the "psychonutrient connection" to help bring mental patients back into the fold of day-to-day living. His book reports on extensive research done in his own clinic and in those of his colleagues in this new and important field. From "hopeless" cases of schizophrenia to common everyday depressions suffered by millions of people, these physicians have found that food sensitivities are often the root cause of their patients' problems. Many of them have been able to return to productive lives. They will need to remain on strict dietary regimens for the rest of their lives, but that seems like a small price to pay to someone who has been living in restraints, behind locked doors for years.

Theron Randolph, M.D., an allergist who laid much of the foundation in establishing a correlation between mental illness and food allergy, is quoted in *Brain Allergies* as saying that "60 to 70 percent of symptoms diagnosed as psychosomatic are in fact undiagnosed maladaptive reactions to foods, chemicals and inhalants."

Philpott continues:

My own practice as a psychiatrist has shown that for 250 consecutive, unselected emotionally disturbed patients, there is convincing evidence that the majority developed major symptoms on exposure to their commonly consumed foods and frequently encountered chemicals. The highest percentage of symptom formation occurred in those diagnosed as psychotic. Ninety-two percent of those classified as schizophrenic developed symptoms as maladaptive reactions to foods and chemicals; 65 percent manifested symptom formation on exposure to wheat; 51 percent manifested symptom formation on exposure to mature corn products; and 51 percent manifested symptom formation on exposure to pasteurized whole cow's milk . . . Some of the reactions in this group were so severe as to precipitate suicidal attempts or delusions.

The emotional symptoms evoked on exposure to foods and commonly met chemicals range from mild central-nervous-system symptoms such as weakness, dizziness, blurred vision, anxiety and depression, to gross psychotic symptoms such as catatonia, dissociation, paranoid delusions and visual and auditory hallucinations. I do not recall any schizophrenic symptom described in medical literature that was not observed in the 250 patients tested; gross psychotic symptoms occurred in a very high percentage.

It's hard to associate a harmless bowl of wheat flakes or a few slices of toast with the violent, self-destructive tendencies of mental illness. Perhaps the severity of the toxic reaction is due to a genetic weakness; or perhaps the sensitivity was so abused over the years that the body's immune system finally gave out. We don't know why some people are so devastated by the foods they eat and others can seemingly abuse their bodies for years with no noticeable problems.

Many instituionalized schizophrenics can be released from their wards when cereal grains and dairy products are removed from their diets. If gluten from wheat is added to their meals, these patients again become ill. Wheat products are certainly not the only substances that cause cerebral symptoms, but, along with dairy and corn, they are high on the list as repeat offenders.

Obviously, if foods that our body distinguishes as toxic to our systems can be responsible for serious mental illness, they certainly can be the cause of many of our everyday mental ailments. Countless numbers of people try to live with their depressions, headaches, inability to learn or concentrate and all the rest, because they feel they should have the strength of character to overcome them. Others will take their tattered emotions to psychiatrists who may prescribe drugs to counter the symptoms, drugs that only mask the symptoms, allowing the person to ignore his body's call for help. This can pave the way for more serious illness, mental or physical.

Symptoms of brain sensitivity are often difficult to detect. Our society conditions us to "be strong" and not let the meanderings of our minds overtake our ability to function in the world. We fight the symptoms by trying to ignore them. We take aspirin for our headaches, and when they grow into migraines, we call the doctor for something stronger. We try to drown our emotions in alcohol or drugs. We adapt to the unhappiness of being disappointed each new day or of feeling a lack of excitement about life itself. When we find we can't concentrate on our work, we simply put the work away or find an excuse not to do it.

Growing numbers of psychiatrists and psychological therapists are recognizing the food and chemical connection to psychoses and are counseling their patients to begin therapy by first isolating their food sensitivities. Many of them are now routinely sending their patients in for Cytotoxic testing to make sure that their work is not hampered by food sensitivities.

HYPOGLYCEMIA AND BRAIN SENSITIVITIES

We are just beginning to realize what astounding numbers of people there are who are afflicted with hypoglycemia, or low blood sugar. Hypoglycemia was recognized as a disease by the medical establishment only a few years ago. Before that, sufferers were told their symptoms were "all in their heads." How could they be so right and so wrong at the same time?

I bring up this illness because its symptoms are often confused with food sensitivities, and it's important to distinguish between the two so proper nutritional measures can be taken.

Harvey Ross, M.D., author of *Hypoglycemia—the Disease Your Doctor Won't Treat,* has treated thousands of cases of hypoglycemia. He also treats patients for food sensitivities, using the Cytotoxic test as a method of isolating them. He takes a careful history from patients complaining of cerebral symptoms, like tiredness, irritability, and confusion, to ascertain whether he's dealing with hypoglycemia or a food sensitivity. The histories usually expose which problem the patient has.

A hypoglycemic will complain of fatigue and lack of energy—both unrelated to the amount of sleep he gets. Most will suffer from significant depressions unrelated to life's events. They often try to reach for reasons that would explain their depression. There are also episodes of anxiety, with rapid heartbeats, fearfulness, all coming on in spurts. Physically, the hypoglycemic may experience headaches and chest, abdominal, or back pain. Confusion and mental cloudiness that clear up after eating are common.

While people with food sensitivities may share many of these symptoms, the hypoglycemic's history will probably show a long-standing sweet tooth or, less frequently, a propensity toward starches. Alcoholism is also quite prevalent among hypoglycemics. A real clue to the difference is that people with food sensitivities often feel worse after eating and great while fasting, unlike the hypoglycemic who gets relief from food.

5

The Food Sensitivity Addiction/Withdrawal/ Craving Syndrome

Ronnie loved pasta. Her hands would shake in anticipation of it the way a nicotine-deprived smoker sometimes shakes when he approaches a cigarette counter, the way a junkie feels a few minutes before his "connection" arrives.

Ronnie would rarely go out to dinner with friends, because she worried that they might want to go someplace that didn't serve her beloved spaghetti. On the rare occasion that she would go for some "foreign" food, her friends would laugh as she predictably picked the item on the menu that most closely resembled pasta.

Raised in a very large, religious Italian family, Ronnie's love of pasta had deep cultural ramifications. True, her obsession was strong, but not as strange as it may at first seem.

Any one of us could probably sit down and write a story similar to Ronnie's, because we all have passionate feelings about some of our favorite foods. I've seen Midwestern ranchers balk at the idea of giving up their cherished beefsteaks, even though their doctors prove to them, beyond a shadow of a doubt, that their systems cannot tolerate more cholesterol, that a heart attack is imminent, if not overdue. One burly 50-year-old, 250-pound Texan slammed his fist down on my desk when I suggested he eliminate beef, dairy, and wheat products for a few months, since they reacted strongly on his Cytotoxic test. "Why, young man, that'd be downright un-American," he declared. And he meant it. As if suffering a fatal heart attack was something akin to dying for his country!

In Ronnie's case, her favorite food, pasta, turned out to be the cause of severe asthma attacks. They were so serious at times that emergency hospitalization was required. Desensitization shots administered by her allergist provided only minor relief.

I met Ronnie, a likable, vivacious attorney, in 1979. We discussed the possibility that foods might be responsible for her condition. She was desperate for some kind of answer, as her asthmatic condition, which at one time had been only seasonal, had suddenly become constant and was getting more and more intense. She agreed to think about taking the Cytotoxic test, but wanted to discuss it with her allergist first.

When she mentioned the possibility of food sensitivity to her doctor, he laughed. She left his office, called me immediately, and came in for the Cytotoxic test. Predictably, her results showed severe reactions to wheat (pasta), tomato, cheese—literally everything she loved to eat.

After seven days of eliminating these foods, she was a different person, able to resume many of her much-loved exercises. After a while she was even able to take up aerobic dancing. Her doctor, upon seeing Ronnie's tremendous improvement, contacted me for more information on the Cytotoxic test.

THE APPLE ADDICT

Cravings are the first link in the addiction chain. Most of us have certain foods we feel we can't live without. When I was younger, I consumed vast quantities of sweets. In college and working part-time, I relied on fast foods and sweets to satisfy my hunger. I spent years surviving on hamburgers and French fries, sweet rolls and sodas. But these were easy to give up compared to my big food addiction—apples.

I would have two or three apples every day and often would top them off with a can or two of applesauce. When my first Cytotoxic test showed a sensitivity to apples, I decided to give them up. I didn't realize how hard it would be to quit after thirty years of eating several apples a day. I was clearly addicted!

It took me years to accept my cravings—apples and others—for what they really were and are: chemical-food addictions. I didn't develop these addictions through any flaw in my character or through an inability to handle stress, as we assume people pick up chemical addictions. I became a food addict the way we all do, innocently, through misinformation and improper encouragement by parents, school, and society. These factors lead to abuse or overuse of foods, which, in turn, can lead to addictions. I was conditioned to respond positively to carefully crafted advertising slogans like "The Great American Hot Dog," or "Chocolate, the Energy Food," and "Everybody Needs Milk."

This last slogan, developed by a large advertising agency for the California Milk Producers Advisory Board, is a prime example of how so many of our nutritional concepts are really nothing more than advertising pitches.

"Everybody Needs Milk" was challenged by the Federal Trade Commission in 1974, according to Frank Osaki, M.D., and John V. Bell in their book, *Don't Drink Your Milk!* A subsequent *New York Times* headline read: "Federal Trade Commission Finds Milk Advertising Campaign Deceptive." The FTC had gathered reams of documentation showing that the vast majority of the world's population is born without the enzyme lactase, required to digest milk and some milk products. "But the dairymen were fast on their feet," write Osaki and Bell. "By the time the Federal Trade Commission had announced its intent to file a complaint, the advertising slogan had already been changed from 'Everybody Needs Milk' to 'Milk Has Something for Everybody.'"

Nevertheless, young people, listening to the ad slogans over and over again, knew nothing about FTC challenges. They continued to believe—and still do—that milk is the perfect food.

I use this case to illustrate the thoroughness with which we are brainwashed into overusing many food substances. It is, say a growing number of experts in the field of food allergy/sensitivity research, the abuse of certain foods that begins the sensitivity/addiction/withdrawal/craving cycle.

The thought of developing withdrawal symptoms over a bowl of spaghetti or French fries or apples may seem absurd. But before shrugging it off, let me suggest that you try eliminating, for only a week, any one of the foods you love enough to eat every day. Quit all wheat products, if you eat a lot of bread, cakes, and pasta. Or stop eating sugar, if you have a sweet tooth; or coffee, if you drink it every day. I am sure your compassion for the cases mentioned in this chapter will grow as you watch your every thought centered around the one food you've given up.

The best example of the food addiction/withdrawal syndrome I can think of is the case of Maria, who knows better than anyone how overpowering food withdrawals can be.

When she was twenty-four years old, Maria was diagnosed as having extreme hypoglycemia. "I think my doctor used the hypoglycemia diagnosis to explain away my horrible migraines, confusion, irrational behavior, and overweight," she recalls, "because there was nothing else to pin my symptoms on. The hypoglycemic diet [rich in proteins, low in sugars and carbohydrates] gave me no relief at all."

She lived with her problem for ten years, when a move from Michigan to Los Angeles put enough additional stress on her body to cause her symptoms to go completely out of control. Everything became more dramatic; the headaches, now constant, were accompanied by continuous vomiting or nausea.

In Los Angeles, a friend was listening to her complaints and asked if she ever went on food binges or felt compulsive about any foods. Maria laughed. Of course, she went on binges all the time. Doesn't everyone? She was serious. Her friend suggested that she might be suffering from food allergies and pointed her in the direction of food allergy specialist Harvey Ross, M.D., who explained that she was probably not hypoglycemic, as food binging usually indicates some other problem.

At Ross's suggestion, she took a Cytotoxic test and reacted to fifty-seven foods (the average number of reactions is thirty-two). Many of the sensitive foods were those included in her hypoglycemic diet, namely dairy products.

Maria prepared carefully for her elimination diet, woke up the next morning determined not to eat any of the foods she reacted to on the test. A few slices of turkey for breakfast, some carrots and celery for lunch; by three in the afternoon, her boss was asking her if she felt all right. Her normally ruddy complexion was pure white. She was tired, she told him, but felt that she could finish the day. By five, he passed her desk again and ordered her to go home immediately, telling her she looked really ill.

At home, exhausted, she managed to down a few more carrot and celery sticks and flopped into bed. The next morning, Maria began her day as usual at 5:00 A.M., showered, and then suddenly realized she didn't have the strength to towel herself dry. Putting her bathrobe over her shoulders, she wandered around her house, ending up in the living room where she sat down and was overcome by uncontrollable sobbing.

"How absurd," she recalls thinking at the time, "This is crazy. I must get my act together right now." But she couldn't move.

Maria is, by her own description, a "mover and shaker." As administrative coordinator and paraprofessional handling her own caseload, she is also litigation supervisor in a thirty-man law firm. She was hating the helplessness she felt as she stared into her closet, unable to make even the simplest decision about what to wear. All she could do was cry.

Incoherent, she couldn't communicate with her office over the telephone. She just slammed down the receiver, went back to her bedroom, pulled the blankets over her head and began three hours of alternating hot sweats and freezing cold shivers. By noon, no longer able to lie, sit or stand still for a minute, she began pacing the floor, drawn to compulsive movement. She couldn't stop moving for the next two days; finally, things began to settle down. Her thought processes started clearing, and in a few days she was able to return to work.

During this entire episode, Maria never once connected her distress to her food eliminations, even though she stuck to her diet throughout. When she returned to work, it was her boss, whose wife had experienced food addiction withdrawals, who pointed out the probable connection.

While her body was grappling with these addictions, Maria experienced strong cravings for dairy products, especially cheese and ice cream. These cravings lasted for about a year. If she gave in to them, she would become violently ill. Now she is able to eat these foods occasionally with only mild symptoms appearing the next day.

After a year and a half on the Food Sensitivity Diet (see Chapter 9), Maria took another Cytotoxic test, which showed that she'd gone down from fifty-seven to forty-two reactions. After three years, she is symptom free as long as she maintains her diet.

"The most dynamic realization I had," Maria told me one day, "was that I always thought I was very smart—scored high on IQ tests and that sort of thing—but after only five days on this diet, I felt like my whole life had been in confusion compared to the way I was now feeling, how clearly and acutely my thought processes had become. My real abilities had been masked all those years."

Chemical-food addiction is a very real, very well-documented medical fact, a fact that proves the age-old adage that too much of any good thing is no good. What we are dealing with is not a psychological problem, although food addictions use the emotions to signal their cravings to the brain. They are a physiological phenomenon. Like a drug or alcohol dependency, the food addiction is based on a chemical disorder in the body; and the addiction process is identical for food, drugs, alcohol, or cigarettes.

To understand this process, consider a tobacco dependency, something with which we are all familiar, either through our own habit or that of a friend. Not everyone is allergic or sensitive to tobacco, according to Cytotoxic test results. This is not to say that tobacco smoke is not harmful to everyone through its tar and nicotine residues and other effects, but it does explain why some people are able to smoke a few cigarettes once in a while and never get "hooked." The rest of us begin to smoke one day and within a week are smoking a pack a day. Before long, we are scheduling our lives around our addiction.

At this stage, our bodies have adapted to the chemical. The addiction is well seated. But how did it get started?

When most people inhale cigarette smoke for the first time, they will have an immediate allergic reaction. Tears may start streaming, or they will cough, gag, get dizzy, and sometimes become nauseated. After the third or fourth cigarette, though, the symptoms start to fade. Nature created the human body to be adaptable to adverse situations so that it can survive under less than optimum conditions. When the smoker persists, the body, in its wisdom, will suppress its response. This is called "specific adaptation," and the disappearance or lessening of the symptom display clears the way for the addiction to take over.

An addiction is nothing more than an adaptation the body makes in order to survive. Obviously, if the body were to keep producing the strong symptoms it did when first introduced to the "foreign" substance—in this case, cigarette smoke—it would expire. So, as it does hundreds of times each day in many different biological and emotional areas, it makes a compromise, an adjustment. It adapts to substandard functioning.

The mistake we make is to confuse the lack of symptoms and the accompanying feeling of well-being with an absence of harmful effects from the cigarette smoke. The body is still reacting to the chemical. The immune system is still being attacked, and white blood cells are dying every time the smoker takes another "drag."

The state of addiction puts the body in a pattern of chronic stress, rendering the immune system weakened when it comes to fighting serious illness. During the addiction the immune system gives up its fight against the substance, begins to adapt to the constant assault, and actually develops a *need* for the substance.

Under normal circumstances, the body will crave what it needs for survival. With an addiction, the body craves what it *thinks* it needs, the result of a confused immune system. The smoker knows that cigarette smoke is harmful to him, yet his response is that he *needs* a drag of nicotine. Every time he inhales some smoke, the immune system sends out its white blood cells, its "soldiers," to attack the foreign substance. It's a sort of suicide mission for the immune system. When the cigarette smoke enters the system on a regular basis, the immune system's "troop buildup" becomes automatic. If the smoker decides to cut down or stop smoking and the regularity of the assault is interrupted, the immune system is actually let down.

Cytotoxic researcher Dr. Geoffrey Cheung compares this letdown to the country in a state of war. Anyone familiar with history knows that wars produce healthy economies. As long as battles rage, the citizens remain involved, motivated, and the soldiers mass their forces against the common enemy. As soon as peace arrives, though, things start falling apart. The economy slows down, troops are mustered out, and millions of civilian workers in the war machine are out on the streets. While a continued state of war would eventually be disastrous, countries come to depend on a war, as we often depend on our addictions, for a sense of balance and direction.

Every recovered alcoholic knows that even one drink can put him right back on the skids, even if he hasn't touched a drop of alcohol for years. The reason for this can also be explained by the Cytotoxic effect. Once the immune system has grown dependent on a substance—be it alcohol, foods, or nicotine—the white blood cells will always remain massed for a possible attack by that substance. Even a drop is enough to stimulate a major immunological attack, but it's not enough to satisfy the body's massive buildup. There is a letdown, and a craving for the substance will follow. The person will feel as if he never stopped drinking.

ALCOHOLISM

Current food allergy research, and especially Cytotoxic research, is beginning to prove that the term alcoholism is a misnomer. In *An Alternative Approach to Allergies,* Drs. Randolph and Moss discuss the plight of the alcoholic, and Cytotoxic test findings certainly prove the doctors' point; that the "alcoholic" may not be addicted to alcohol at all. The root of his addiction is most often the *grain* that his favorite drinks are made from; or perhaps brewers' yeast, which is used in all alcoholic beverages; or the grapes that are used in wine. In fact, since breweries and wineries are not required to label their products with ingredients, there are many additives, sugars, flavor enhancers, and other things used in hard liquor, beer, and wines. (See the Appendix for more information.)

Almost without exception, the bourbon drinker's Cytotoxic test will show a sensitivity to corn, the Scotch drinker's to barley or malt, as these are the principal components of such drinks. Drs. Randolph and Moss call alcoholism the "acme or pinnacle of the food-addiction pyramid."

The alcoholic who quits drinking but doesn't eliminate the grains or other food substances to which he is sensitive will never lose his cravings for alcohol. Unknowingly, he is still feeding his addiction, and making his life more difficult than it need be. It would be easier by far to isolate the offending grains, yeast, or grapes and eliminate them totally from the diet. This is sure to quiet the cravings once and for all.

VITAMINS AND DRUGS

While many drugs, like heroin, codeine, amphetamines, and Valium, are noted for their addictive qualities, Cytotoxic research shows that any chemical, when taken into the body every day, can cause a sensitivity to develop. This holds true for drugs and vitamin tablets, as well as food substances. Peering through our microscopes, we can see the Cytotoxic effect working on many facets of our lives.

I wouldn't dream of suggesting that a person stop taking drugs prescribed by his medical doctor, but I would caution anyone to be on the alert when taking prescription drugs that may not be life-or-death necessities. If your body has become sensitized to them, they may be doing you more harm than good.

An example would be birth control pills. Many women on the pill complain of severe dysmenorrhea (painful menstrual periods) or PMS (premenstrual syndrome). This happens so often that doctors should probably suggest that they eliminate the pill for a few months before trying any other treatment. Often, these women have been taking birth control pills for years. Their bodies have built up sensitivities to the pills and are signaling the problem through the pain or depression symptoms.

And then there is our national preoccupation with vitamins. Think about the billions of vitamin pills we take every year. Americans are absolutely fanatical about popping vitamins—something I consider an adjunct to our culture's "quick fix" obsession. We spend billions of dollars on vitamins, yet we rarely take the time to analyze or research the substances we are taking. Many thousands of us are doing more harm than good with the vitamins we take. While we may not build up a sensitivity to the nutrients themselves, we know that many of our most popular vitamins are based on two of the most sensitive substances for most of us—yeast and corn. In addition, many of us are sensitive to the foods that natural vitamins are derived from, like the fish-liver oils that give us much of our vitamins A and D, the egg shells that provide calcium. Milk products are often used as fillers in vitamin tablets. These are a few examples of the ways in which vitamins can actually be the vehicles for harmful substances entering the body. It is possible to purchase vitamins with very clearly marked ingredient labels that will tell you exactly what is contained in the tablets. One sure way to avoid abusing vitamins is to consult with a nutritionally-oriented physician.

AVOIDING ADDICTIONS

A food or chemical cannot become addictive if it is not consumed or taken too often. Just how often is "too often" can be determined only by your own physiology and emotional make-up. When people use the Food Sensitivity Diet (see Chapter 9) to eliminate their food sensitivities, we suggest rotating the foods they are eating so that no food is eaten more than once every four days. This is sometimes difficult to achieve at first because we tend to develop habitual eating routines. But as hard as it may seem, the best way to avoid the addictive process is to vary every aspect of your diet as much as possible, eliminating entirely the foods you crave.

Isn't it about time that we became the masters instead of the slaves when it comes to what foods enter or don't enter our bodies?

6

Food Sensitivities in Infants and Children

Awaiting the birth of her first child, Ardith Berger was kept awake at night by her unborn baby's incessant rolling and kicking inside her. An active fetus, the doctor smiled; nothing to worry about. She was having a normal pregnancy, except for the morning sickness that followed her through seven months of pregnancy and except for the false labor she experienced during her seventh month. These things were nothing unusual, though, and her delivery was easy.

The baby, Alisa, was bright, healthy, and cranky. Prone to clenching her little fists and toes, she would stiffen her body and scream for hours on end. The family pediatrician told the new parents not to worry, that their baby was probably teething.

Like most new mothers in the late 1960s, Ardith wasn't encouraged to breastfeed. She didn't want sagging breasts, and she didn't want to take the extra time off from work. Anyway, her doctor told her that infant formulas were at least as good if not better for baby than breast milk. But Alisa had a difficult time adapting to formula. Evenings were particularly trying, as that was when Alisa's "teething" crankiness would flare up. Peaceful dinners were relegated to the fond-memory file.

However rocky her first months, Alisa soon grew into a bright, happy, albeit slightly overweight child. What her parents and pediatrician didn't know is that Alisa's prenatal and postnatal symptoms were clear indications of severe food sensitivities.

Her symptoms disappeared right after babyhood and remained relatively dormant (except for a slight weight problem) until just after her eleventh birthday. Then they reappeared and put her through a kind of living hell, a situation that took her through four of Los Angeles's leading psychiatrists, a neuropsychiatric unit at a major university, and a variety of clinical psychologists who gave her batteries of psychological tests. All this in the span of less than a year. Her bewildered parents found themselves on the brink of institutionalizing their heretofore normal, happy child. The only thing that kept them from listening to their doctors' advice was a sheer determination and belief that there was nothing mentally wrong with her.

No one could tell Alisa's story better than she, so here it is, as she recorded it, with only a few changes for clarity:

> In the sixth grade I didn't have a very good year. My grades were falling and people didn't like me because I was fat and didn't feel very good. I really thought I was mental, but my Mom said no. At school when the teacher would talk, I would hear her but what she said just didn't go through. I talked to my teacher about it and then my Mom, who took me to our pediatrician for a checkup. He checked me and gave me a blood test and said my problem was probably anxiety and told Mom to take me to a psychiatrist.
>
> I was starting to have fights with everyone, and my school and teachers and homework all seemed wrong to me. I thought they were all ganging up on me.

I remember May 20, 1981, because that's when I had my first seizure. Mom said my pupils dilated and I remember that the light made me feel worse. Inside of me I felt like two people—a mean person, a bad guy, and another person who would try and help me. The bad guy would tell me to hurt other people and myself. He would tell me to kill myself. Sometimes I would feel like I was flying or that I was on a railroad track. I would drool, fall down and faint, or hit someone.

It got to where I could set it off myself by staring in the mirror at my eyes. Once I started, I couldn't talk, only write notes. My Mom would throw paper at me so I could write and tell her what to do. At school, I would get bad stomach aches and pains in my legs. Then I knew one of those seizures was coming on. I would call my parents to pick me up, and as soon as I got in the car, it would start. I wouldn't always remember what I did, but sometimes I did remember and it really scared me to think about it. Once I got up in the middle of the night and ran ten blocks in my pajamas. Another time, I had a seizure in the swimming pool at night. I was alone and couldn't call for help, but I managed to get out of the water. Then I just fainted on the cement. I guess my parents carried me inside; I don't remember.

My Mom and Dad tried everything they could to get me to stop. I know the doctors weren't giving them many good ideas, so they were sort of all on their own. Daddy once threw water on me. Another time I slapped him as hard as I could and he slapped me back. They would lock me in my room, or try to talk me out of it. The doctors gave them drugs to give me, but nothing worked, nothing.

The seizures would last for hours, and I was getting them almost every day, sometimes twice a day for about six months. The first psychiatrist said I was showing my anger because Mom and Dad had such a loving relationship and didn't fight. He figured I never learned to express my anger and this was my way of doing it.

I was going to see him three times a week, and people told me he was the most famous psychiatrist in Los Angeles. But nothing was helping. One night I got so

bad that my parents tried to hospitalize me in a psychi-
atric ward. They tested me for drugs at the hospital,
because I guess I looked like I was on drugs or something. Another doctor did a bunch of personality tests
and told my parents that I was severely emotionally
disturbed and had a low IQ and needed even more
therapy.

That's when our psychiatrist told Mom he couldn't
see me anymore because I was too disturbed. He said I
needed even more sessions than I was having, and
since my parents didn't have medical insurance, he figured they couldn't afford to pay him more money. I
know they were already spending $85 a session three
times a week. The doctor said he didn't have time to
work with me on a reduced-fee basis.

Mom cried. Daddy was sick in the hospital with a virus. But when he got home he found this article in his
Penthouse magazine about food allergies and mental
illness. It listed the Academy of Orthomolecular Psychiatry in New York as a source of information. My
parents stayed up all night and called New York first
thing in the morning. They gave us Dr. Ross's number
in L.A.

I didn't believe what Dr. Ross was saying about food
sensitivities maybe causing my problems, but Mom
was happy to hear him say he thought he could help.
No one had said those words for a very long time. I
took a Cytotoxic test and it showed that I was sensitive
to everything I was eating. What a shock. I reacted to
forty-three out of one hundred fifty foods, and many of
them were really bad reactions. Milk, every kind of
sugar, beef, lots of fruits and vegetables, corn. My favorite food was Mexican food, and I turned out to be
sensitive to every single ingredient and spice they use.

I went on the Cytotoxic diet, eliminating all the
foods that showed up on the test. The reactions started
slowing down. In a month even my stomach aches
went away. If I cheated—I remember eating an ice
cream once—I would start getting a reaction right
away. I'd get angry, slam doors. The "bad guy" came
right back. Scary.

But Dr. Ross felt sure that at some point my body

would be able to handle most of those foods, and I tried some of them after a few months went by, but my symptoms came right back. Every month we would try some of the foods that showed only slight reactions on the Cytotoxic test, but it was a whole year before I could eat any of them at all without having my symptoms come back. Then I was finally able to start eating small amounts of all my old foods, and now I can tolerate just about anything I want.

I still never know if the "bad guy" will ever come back again. But I guess it's different now, because I would know what to do. So it's not that scary to me anymore.

I can't imagine what Alisa's parents must have gone through in sticking to their intuitive feelings. Perhaps the fact that their daughter had never displayed any emotional problems before the onset of these seizures gave them a clue that there was nothing mentally wrong. By the same token, though, I wonder why all her doctors took no notice of that fact. Fortunately, there are now doctors and organizations across the country who believe that food sensitivities are at the root of many childhood ailments.

Alisa is, at this writing, thirteen years old. She is now enjoying life, easily maintaining an honor status at school and worrying over the kinds of things all teenagers worry about. She no longer wakes up with night terrors, no longer doubts her sanity. She agreed to work with us on this book because she believes there are probably many children suffering as she did, children who don't have a bit of information on the causes of their problems or a ghost of a chance of curing themselves.

Alisa's instincts are quite accurate. There are an alarming number of schoolchildren operating far below their capacities due to food sensitivities. Current estimates of children suffering from behavior and learning problems run as high as 10 percent of the total child population. A more conservative figure, reported by J. J. Bosco and S. S. Robin, is between 1 and 3 percent. And these are only the cases that are noticed and reported! What about the twelve-year-old who gets fifteen hours of sleep at night and is still tired all day? Or the child who could be getting A's in school but barely passes his courses because his brain is too fuzzy to think well? Or the young girl who feels angry all the time, too angry ever to make a friend? These and many, many others are the undiagnosed, misunderstood cases. The intolerant foods they eat are keeping their young systems from digesting and assimilating whatever other nutritious foods they may be getting. Their brains are virtually starving, and their bodies and minds are suffering. The symptoms may be nowhere as harsh or apparent as Alisa's, but they are there, nevertheless, in the colicky baby, the cranky toddler, the hyperactive child, the underachieving, restless teenager.

A very sad aspect of this problem is that there are thousands, maybe millions of loving parents unknowingly aggravating their children's symptoms. Sometimes, when parents discover that foods are causing problems in their children, they feel tremendous guilt for having provided these foods. It's terribly important for parents to realize that research on food reactions is very new. And while the Cytotoxic test finally gives doctors and nutritionists an easy way to help isolate offending foods, there is no way parents could have known about this phenomenon even a decade ago.

We must put our feelings aside and be glad this information is now available. The guilt will soon give way to astonishment at the turnaround we see in our children once offending foods are isolated and removed from their diets. When given half a chance, the body is a miraculous recoverer. Often, within a few days, there is a dramatic reduction in symptoms, a clarity in thinking, and a new feeling of well-being.

Symptom Chart

Below is a listing, taken in part from Dr. Lendon Smith's *Food for Healthy Kids*, of many common symptoms of food sensitivities in pregnant and lactating women, in babies and in children. Many of these symptoms can also signal nutrient deficiencies or other physiological problems, so a nutritionally oriented medical doctor or a nutritionist should be consulted. It's extremely important to make sure that mother and baby are receiving enough vitamins and minerals during pregnancy and nursing and that young children receive the special supplements they may need. If extra nutrients and other common sense dietary precautions don't work (lowering the intake of sugars and refined carbohydrates, eliminating alcoholic beverages and cigarettes during pregnancy and while nursing), there are probably food sensitivities present.

Prenatal and Lactation (Mothers)
- Morning sickness
- Gas
- Fatigue
- Swollen ankles or other localized edema
- Headaches
- Food cravings
- Overactive uterine activity
- Increased inhalant allergies or sinus activity
- Joint aches
- Insufficient breast milk
- Depression or confusion

Babies
- Rashes
- Cradle cap
- Colic
- Wakefulness at night (although many breast-fed babies wake often at night because breast milk is so easily absorbed by their bodies that they get hungry more often than bottle-fed babies)
- Incessant rocking
- Constant motion
- Stuffy nose
- Gas
- Ear infections
- Bronchial infections
- Touchiness—doesn't want to be held

Children
- Headaches
- Stomach aches

- Joint pains
- Muscle pains
- Anal itching or burning
- Stinging during urination
- Skin rashes
- Inability to concentrate
- Fearfulness, fatigue, depression
- Prone to chills
- Clearer thinking during certain times of the day
- Cloudy thinking after meals
- Craves sweets, milk, breads, or other foods
- Dark circles under eyes
- Paleness
- Eczema
- Dandruff
- Cracks behind ears
- Acne
- Squinting or red, itchy eyes
- Large pupils
- Night terrors
- Wandering around at night, sleepwalking
- Bed-wetting
- Excessive urination
- Mucous in nose or throat
- Rapid pulse
- Cold, moist palms
- Bad breath
- Passing smelly gas
- Unusual odor in urine

PRENATAL FOOD SENSITIVITIES

The food sensitivity cycle starts way before a baby is born. While in the womb, he depends on his mother's digestive system for all his nutrition. Along with the foods, he also receives the food sensitivities. Until recently, it was assumed that only nutrients and healthy substances could pass through the placenta walls and reach the unborn child. It's true that the placental barrier maintains a relatively pure environment for the fetus, but researchers now understand that the IgG immunoglobulin does cross the placental barrier. As a matter of fact, it is the only immunoglobulin that can cross. IgG is necessary for the fetus because it provides the baby with immunity against infections the mother may be contacting or harboring in her body. But this is also the same serum protein that is called into action by the immune system when there is a food sensitivity. In simple terms, the same IgG that has been reacting to a food sensitivity in the mother, and is therefore now elevated in her blood, easily crosses the placental barrier and starts reacting on the fetus.

During the digestive process, the mother's system often fails to break down foodstuffs adequately. This causes large molecules to pass to the fetus. These macromolecules get into the blood stream and are attacked by the IgG immunoglobulin because of their large size. The attacking white cells explode in the Cytotoxic effect and their powerful enzymes are released in the womb, starting the sensitization syndrome in the baby.

The fetus can also receive a food sensitivity by ingesting large quantities of certain food substances that enter the placenta, or he may have inherited a sensitivity to the particular food genetically.

Certainly there are babies born with a propensity toward allergies and sensitivities. Leading doctors in the field of food allergy research point to a genetic lack of specific enzymes in some individuals that makes it difficult if not impossible for them to digest certain foods. If there is not a complete lack of the enzyme, there could be a decreased amount of it, or even a malfunction in the production of the enzyme—all of which could account for a substandard digestive system and the onset of food sensitivities.

Pediatrician Lendon Smith, author of a number of best-selling books on baby and childhood nutrition, points out that pregnant and nursing women should try to rotate the foods they are eating whenever possible to avoid creating food sensitivities in their unborn children or in themselves. Rotating the diet means never eating the same food more than once every four days, as it takes about four to five days for the body to process some foods fully (see Chapter 10).

SENSITIVITIES AND THE NEWBORN

Once the baby is born, of course, symptoms are more noticeable. If he has rashes or frequent colic, has trouble nursing because his nose is stuffed up, or if he displays any of the symptoms listed on the Symptom Chart (pp. 53–54), chances are food sensitivities are impairing his immune system. While breast-feeding is the best way to avoid allergic reactions in a newborn, there are food sensitivities that can pass through the mother's system to her milk. Douglas E. Johnstone, M.D., reported in 1981 in the Annals of Allergy on a 1978 study of nineteen breast-fed infants with severe colic. When the mothers eliminated cow's milk from their diet, the colic disappeared in thirteen of the eighteen infants. In twelve of these thriteen, the colic reappeared when the mothers resumed drinking milk. Nursing mothers are usually encouraged by their doctors to drink large quantities of cow's milk; it's an easy way to fill their needs for extra calcium and protein. Yet Cytotoxic testing shows consistently high percentages of sensitivities to dairy products. When we compare Cytotoxic test results, cow's milk shows up as the number-one sensitivity.

Many medical doctors staunchly deny any connection between a mother's diet and the quality of her breast milk. They must think the mother's body has an entirely independent milk-generating plant that reacts to none of the foods she eats. Current research clearly shows this to be a foolish notion.

I remember one puzzled mother telling me that her breast-fed baby boy had bad stomach aches several times a week, for no apparent reason. His episodes always came on the days she would meet her friends for breakfast at a neighborhood delicatessen, and she figured that the excitement at the restaurant was too much stress for her three-month-old. She laughed and said, "Well, it sure couldn't be my pickle fetish." She admitted loving pickles with a passion, sometimes eating five or six in one sitting and then taking a bag of them home to munch on. It was an obvious connection, and her Cytotoxic test corroborated it; she was highly sensitive to both cucumbers and vinegar. As soon as she eliminated pickles from her diet, her baby's colic disappeared.

In bottle-fed babies, when there is a problem, the first thing to identify is a possible allergy or sensitivity to cow's milk. Switching to raw goat's milk or soy milk is often helpful, but again, remember to rotate, because sometimes the sensitivity isn't to the milk at all, but to sugar or other ingredients in the formula mixture. Some experimenting may be necessary.

CHILDHOOD

By the time a baby is introduced to his first solid food, he may have a number of food sensitivities already at work. To my mind, many mothers switch their babies from breast or formula to cow's milk way too early—sometimes as soon as six months. The mother may soon discover that her baby has come down with a cold or ear infection or is constipated or full of rashes. In the food sensitive baby, intolerant foods attack his immune system and lower his resistance to all kinds of infections. Nutritionally— oriented pediatricians are beginning to advise parents to hold off the introduction of solid foods for at least a year to give the baby's intestines a chance to reach the maturity required to process most foods.

There are some very good books on the market today to help guide parents during this important time. A few of them are noted in the back of this book (p. 180). The only additional advice I can offer is to start rotating your baby's foods as soon as possible. If you try puréed carrots as a first food, introduce it once, then stick with breast milk or formula (fortified with iron) for the rest of the week. Next week, try another food, then breast milk or formula for four more days. When baby is eating some kind of solid food every day, make sure he doesn't eat the same one more than once every four days. This rotating of foods will keep the child from developing sensitivities and will also be of great help in monitoring him for adverse food reactions. Remember, sensitivities are often caused by overconsuming a particular food.

When the two- or three-year-old begins to complain of headaches, stomach aches, or a stuffed nose; when he starts appearing overly restless with jerky, inappropriate movements; when he displays any of the symptoms listed on the Symptom Chart (pp. 53–54), the chances are that a food sensitivity has begun. It's difficult to handle a three-year-old's diet, because he is beginning to have a definite say about what he eats. He will often rebel against certain foods, and he soon discovers that he can get a rise out of Mommy and Daddy by being finicky or by not eating. Parents and relatives may placate the child's whinings or minuscule food intake by giving him sweets or refined nonfoods. This is a dangerous precedent. With each nonnutritious treat, a good vitamin-packed food is left aside, causing a lack of nutrients. Without proper vitamins, especially the B vitamins, the child's already tiny appetite is ruined, and the nutrient lack also puts stress on the glands responsible for producing the important enzymes needed for proper food digestion.

With this in mind, we can see clearly how the parents' concern and love, expressed by offering the child these nonnutritious sweets, can be the beginning of a vicious cycle. More sweets, less real food. Less food containing critical vitamins, less enzyme production. Less enzymes, less digestion and assimilation of real nutrients. Worse yet, sweets, snacks, and most breakfast cereals are loaded with certain ingredients—especially sugar—that actually deplete the body's supply of vitamins. Look around. Aren't many children, maybe even *most* children, hooked on sugar?

This overconsumption of nonfoods leaves plenty of room for the Cytotoxic effect to set in. The additional psychological aspects of rewarding a child's stubbornness with sweets are far-reaching, starting with childhood hyperkinesis, extending to teenage disorders, adult dependencies and neuroses—to say nothing of overweight conditions.

BRAIN FOOD SENSITIVITIES IN CHILDREN

Besides a propensity toward colds and viruses and the obvious headaches and stomachaches, childhood food sensitivities often manifest themselves in cerebral dysfunctions. According to *Allergies and the Hyperactive Child,* by Doris J. Rapp, M.D., there are an estimated four to five million children with learning disabilities and hyperactivity in our schools today. Some children seemingly outgrow these childhood maladies, but in my opinion they may turn into other symptoms as life progresses, perhaps becoming masked for a few years at a time and then reemerging as some other monster, like migraine headaches, ulcers, drug dependencies. A 1974 study by Maurice Bowerman, in fact, estimates that 75 percent of prison inmates were hyperactive children.

Cerebral symptoms from intolerant foods often cause a child to be unable to concentrate or to have a short attention span. He may be unable to complete a chore or even to sit through an entire television show. He's often clumsy, can't be disciplined, and may seem depressed and angry much of the time. Other children don't like him because he's hard to be with.

Hyperactivity is a confusing phenomenon and difficult to diagnose. Many normally active toddlers exhaust their parents with their antics, but the hyperactive child will simply be unable to relax at all. The child is wild, restless, and impossible to manage. His parents find themselves making excuses for him to friends and at school. Hyperactive children are often placed on drugs like Ritalin, Dexedrine, or Cylert. Amphetamines are also routinely used. Isn't it paradoxical that these medications are the very drugs used by adults for the opposite effect? They supposedly calm the young child and are prescribed in about

10 percent of the dosage an adult would use. These drugs often seem to hold things together enough for a hyperactive child to function at school, but they only mask the symptoms. The child's body is crying out for help. The drug buries the symptom, and the body's cries are silenced. But the food sensitivities, the intolerances to environmental chemicals or to food colorings, additives, preservatives—whatever it is that might be causing the symptoms—continue to undermine his body in a Cytotoxic effect or allergic reaction, invisibly paving the way for future illness. Only the discovery and elimination of the substance will truly help the child. If your child is taking one of these drugs at this time, and you wish to experiment with isolating his food sensitivities, it's important to work with a nutritionally oriented medical doctor.

A 1981 study (unpublished) relating food sensitivities to children with Attention Deficit Disorder with Hyperactivity used the Cytotoxic test to isolate the children's intolerant foods.

One of the researchers, Dr. Everett Hughes, explained the difficulty he had in arranging for test subjects. Pediatricians sent him their most hopeless cases. Three special state-funded schools for hyperactive children were contacted to participate. Two of the three schools flatly refused to participate in the study, saying their drug therapy and behavior modification techniques were adequate. One school, however, agreed wholeheartedly to work on the study. In all, thirteen children participated. Only one girl took part. (Lendon Smith states that hyperactivity occurs in a ratio of five boys to one girl, but feels this could be explained by the fact that a boy's hyperactive motor behavior is more obvious than a girl's more verbal hyperactive behavior.) Almost one-third of the children were adopted. There is a high incidence of hyperactivity among adopted children, and I feel it may be due to their never having had, in most cases, the benefit of breast-feeding.

A comprehensive diary was kept on everything the children ate for a week, and then they ate no food at all for a one- to two-week span, except for a hypoallergenic nutritional mixture called Vivonex Standard, or CDD. After the fast, the children were given tests, one of which was a Cytotoxic test. The

Cytotoxic results were given to the children's mothers, who started their children on a diet composed only of foods that hadn't shown up as being reactive on the Cytotoxic test.

The results of the study's follow-up period of four to twelve months varied from subject to subject. Six of the thirteen children controlled their diets, experienced major improvement in their behavioral syndrome, and required no medication. Three other subjects achieved partial food control but returned to their medication. Four subjects failed to control their diets and resumed their medications. In a two-year follow-up to the study, the USC researchers found that about half the children continued to control their diets by rotating the foods they were eating. They remained drug free and were back in regular school programs. The paper concluded, therefore, that 75 percent of the subjects in this limited study responded favorably to a Cytotoxic test program.

An interesting fact that arose from the study's results is that two of the subjects who participated had been following the dietary regimen set forth by Dr. Ben Feingold, who gained national attention a few years ago as the doctor who found that food additives have a physiological connection with hyperactivity in children. His much publicized view that this condition is due mainly to artificial food colorings, flavors, additives, and preservatives and natural salicylates (found in many fruits) led Congress to expand labeling requirements on children's foods to include these substances. He noted that there are more than twenty-seven hundred such substances added to our foods— seventeen different chemicals in artificial pineapple alone. The "Feingold diet" for hyperactive children has drawn rave reviews from many quarters; but strangely enough, the Cytotoxic tests on these two children showed no reaction whatsoever to seven or eight of the foods they had been avoiding on their Feingold diets. During the study, the researchers gave these substances to the children as a "challenge" to their Feingold diets, and they were monitored for reactions. None were noted. They have now reintroduced these substances as part of a regular, controlled diet plan and regret that they had been led to avoid them before. Once again, we find proof of our nutritional individuality. Dr. Feingold did a great deal of pioneering work and helped thousands of hyperactive children by having them eliminate certain substances from their diets. But any blanket diet that seeks to correct symptoms in masses of people is doomed to failure, because it fails to take into account individual differences.

FOOD SENSITIVITIES
AND THE TEENAGER

The child grows into puberty, his hormones are activated, and a substantial new stress is added to his existing load. Once this threshold is crossed, a host of new symptoms may suddenly appear. His babyhood crankiness and stomach problems disappeared during elementary school; now he finds himself covered with acne.

The young girl turns fifteen and is suddenly ten pounds overweight. She is so tired she can hardly keep her eyes open in class and daydreams her way through the entire tenth grade.

Cerebral symptoms seem to manifest themselves strongly during the teenage years, the very years young people are generally abusing their bodies with junk foods and sometimes drugs and cigarettes. Cola and doughnuts for breakfast, hamburgers and French fries for lunch, pizza for dinner. These are the years that food sensitivity/addiction cycles really get started and often last a lifetime if not identified and curtailed. Grain sensitivities can turn into alcoholism; edema and bloating can set the stage for a lifetime of laziness, bad self-image, and excessive weight gain.

I honestly believe that the sanity of many teachers and parents would be saved if young people routinely took a Cytotoxic test when they entered their junior-high-school years. Their schools could offer courses explaining the possibilities of controlling overpowering emotions and physical misery through nutritional awareness. I know it's a pipe dream, but no teenager enjoys feeling lousy, uptight, unwanted, fat, or ugly.

I've worked with many young people who have taken the Cytotoxic test. Once they get past the initial withdrawal period, they get to watch their pimples disappear, their weight become normalized, their moods lighten up, and their ability to concentrate and think in school improve enormously. If they slide on the diet during the first month or so, when they are supersensitive, their symptoms come right back tenfold. I call this nature's way of providing initiative to continue being good to your body.

With adequate vitamin and mineral intake, which can occur regularly in their diets, their bodies start to rebuild, and they can begin eating most of their old foods on a rotating basis after a few months. There will be a difference though. They will no longer crave sugar or caffeine, doughy wheat products or salt. A doughnut for breakfast will look as appetizing as a mud pie, and a sip of cola will be met with a wrinkled nose and lots of "yuks." I've seen it happen many times.

If parents are supportive, the process has a great chance of success. As a parent, support your child by doing it yourself! Preparing treats from the recipe ideas in Chapter 10 will help satisfy the munchies for the whole family, while providing many essential vitamins and minerals.

Alexander Schauss has done a significant amount of research into the connection between food substances and teenage disorders. Some of his findings are astounding, like his studies on milk in relation to juvenile delinquency. In his book, *Diet, Crime and Delinquency,* he reports on a fourteen-year-old boy who was expelled from school after a string of behavior problems that culminated in an attack on a school official. The boy's behavior was unpredictable: he would be violent at times and at others would be good enough to be awarded "school student of the month." He took medication for occasional seizures, and his diet included seven glasses of milk a day. When he eliminated milk, he had no seizures for a week. Then he drank half a gallon and had four seizures that same afternoon. He repeated the process several times, seemingly needing to convince

himself of the connection. Then he quit, never to have a seizure again.

It's sad that the connection between diet and teenage disorders is largely ignored. When a baby has a problem, there are
pediatricians today who will take a nutritional approach.
Adults are beginning to connect their ailments with nutrition
and are consulting their refrigerators and food pantries more
and more to find the answers. But, sadly, teenagers' problems
are almost always shrugged off as being typical teenage growing pains.

THE NEW BREED OF PEDIATRICIAN

Jay Gordon, M.D., and Paul Fleiss, M.D., Los Angeles pediatricians, have a separate room in their reception area for babies
and children who are ill and who might be contagious. They
share a large practice, but the "sick baby room" is rarely occu-
pied. Statistics show that for the size of their practice, they
should have had at least five crib deaths among their patients
during the last few years. They have had none. Their patients,
ranging in age from newborn to twenty years, are astonishingly healthy. The doctors never prescribe drugs for hyperactive
children, asserting their belief that many childhood maladies
arise from nutritional disorders, chief among them food sensitivities.

Dr. Gordon explains: "Food sensitivities and nutritional deficiencies relating to childhood illness is as obvious as anything
could be. If you take a potent drug, it will have systemic effects. The cardiovascular, respiratory, GI, and renal systems
may all be affected by the drug. By the same token, if you ingest, say, walnuts or yogurt, and your body doesn't have the
ability to handle these foods, many of your systems will be affected in a negative way. When we deny this process, we
sound as foolish as those who once thought there was nothing
on earth smaller than a grain of sand. Then someone discov-

ered germs, and surgeons who at one time scoffed at washing their hands before surgery began to scrub everything to avoid infection."

Drs. Gordon and Fleiss are among a small but growing group of medical professionals around the world who would rather check out what's going on in their patients' refrigerators than prescribe drugs to relieve symptoms. The Cytotoxic test is being used increasingly in pediatric practices to help these doctors read the often crippled immune systems of their patients.

7

The Controversy

The Cytotoxic test, when performed by highly skilled and well-trained technicians, provides the first easy way to isolate foods an individual's physiology cannot tolerate. But the Cytotoxic testing procedure is relatively new, and like any other new medical approach, it has come under close scrutiny by the medical and scientific communities.

Scientific evaluation of new procedures is an important aspect of the advancement of medical technology. It sows the seeds of growth and inspires us to strive for perfection, a goal we never reach, but one we constantly strive to meet. Through close scrutiny by scientists, the validity of medical procedures can be proven—to a degree. Studies are conducted, data are collected, and the credibility of the method is documented.

But there is a fine line between the endeavors of dedicated research scientists and physicians who seek to distinguish the validity of new medical procedures and concepts and the stubborn protestations of those medical professionals who will discredit anything that threatens their own accepted methods.

Recently, a number of research scientists, biochemists, medical doctors, nutritionists, and others have dedicated their time to exploring the potential scope of the Cytotoxic effect. At the same time, the American Medical Association and the American Academy of Allergists have raised questions about the Cytotoxic test.

Contention #1:
THE TEST DOES NOT
ACCURATELY ISOLATE ALLERGIES

The major complaint we hear from immunologists, allergists, and other medical professionals is that there is no scientific basis for believing that the Cytotoxic test is a credible procedure for isolating food and/or inhalant allergies.

To this I can only say, they are absolutely right! The Cytotoxic test does not accurately isolate food or inhalant allergies, nor is it meant to. Food allergies affect only about 3 to 7 percent of the population. A person who has an allergy to a food is well aware of the problem and rarely needs a test to prove it. His reactions to the foods he's allergic to are immediate and severe, like an outbreak of hives after eating shrimp, or cramping, vomiting, or diarrhea in response to a milk allergy. An allergic reaction is an entirely different physical phenomenon from a food sensitivity, which is what we are dealing with through the Cytotoxic test.

Food sensitivities do not produce the immediate hypersensitization symptoms that allergies produce. Instead, symptoms of food sensitivities are hidden, masked, occult, or delayed reactions. They can appear anywhere from two hours to a few days after the food is ingested, the symptoms can be pronounced or subtle, and they can change from day to day. The significance of the food sensitivity is its prevalence. While only a tiny percentage of the world's population suffers from food allergies, evidence strongly suggests that we *all* have food sensitivities. More than twenty thousand people have taken Cyto-toxic tests at Physicians Laboratories of California alone, and never has any one of them been free of food sensitivities. In case after case, when a person eliminates these foods from his diet, he will feel better in any number of ways. And if he does have inhalant or food allergies, he often finds that they are at least subdued after his sensitivities have been eliminated.

Contention #2:
THE TEST IS TOO
SUBJECTIVE TO BE RELIABLE

Like most new medical testing procedures, the Cytotoxic test is subjective in that its interpretation depends on the skill of the technician reading the slides. Not so long ago, all blood tests were subjective, including the Complete Blood Count (CBC) routinely given during physical examinations and of crucial importance to people about to have surgery. After a while, the CBC process was automated, so its interpretation was no longer dependent upon the eye of the technician. Before automation, though, if even one red cell was counted wrong, the entire test was thrown off significantly enough to sometimes cause misdiagnoses.

Complete automation of the Cytotoxic test is on the way. We have thus far been able to automate all aspects of the test except the physical reading of the slides, which is still done by a technician. To assure the test's credibility, we go to great lengths to keep our technicians performing at their optimum levels. They are all college graduates with science degrees or they have been trained at the University of Washington School of Medicine's Cytotoxic training lab in St. Louis by the origina-tors of the Cytotoxic test, Dr. William T. K. Bryan and Marian Bryan. After they begin reading slides on their own, they are tested by our staff every week, either by having their work ob-served by our staff scientists or by being given two tubes of blood from the same person, each one labeled differently. The two tubes should, and did, have almost the same results. (A time lapse will cause changes in the blood's composition, so there will never be an exact duplication of results.) So while the Cytotoxic test is still in its subjective stage, we take every precaution to be sure that our technicians are doing the best possible job.

Contention #3:
THE TEST DOESN'T REPRODUCE

Actually, despite what we are led to believe, very few medical tests on live tissue reproduce 100 percent. To illustrate our point, we conducted an informal experiment. At 9:00 A.M., we drew blood from four people who had been fasting for twelve hours and sent their blood samples to a national laboratory for chemistries complete blood counts (C.B.C.). They still hadn't eaten by noon, when we drew their blood again; we sent these additional samples to the same lab, labeled with names different from the morning's batch. The results came back the next day, showing a wide disparity in the test results between the first and second tests.

We cannot fault the lab for this lack of reproducibility. We know for a fact that they use only the most modern, automated equipment and that their technicians are top-notch. It's simply that even the CBC, a medically accepted, scientifically "proven" blood test, doesn't reproduce. It can't, not as long as it is reading live cells, for living matter is always changing. The Cytotoxic test is no different.

What is reproducibility? There are three kinds of testing reproduction we look for. First, when two tubes of blood from the same subject, each labeled with a different name, are given to the same technician, there should be little difference between the first and second tests, providing that little time has lapsed between the first and second test.

Second, when two tubes of blood from the same person are given to two different technicians and they read their slides at approximately the same time, there should be little disparity between their test results.

In the first kind of test, our technicians show a 92 percent reproducibility. In the second type of test, they will have identical test results 85 percent of the time.

Chart highlighting aspects
of experimental test results
comparing sixteen Chemistry and CBC tests

Test	Results Test No. 1	Results Test No. 2	% Change
WBC	6.1×10^3 cells/cc	9.0×10^3 cells/cc	−32%
RBC	4.32×10^6 cells/cc	4.38×10^6 cells/cc	−1.4%
Hbg	13.7 gm/100 ml.	14.2 gm/100 ml	−3.5%
Polys	59%	67%	−11.9%
Lymphs	31%	27%	+14.8%
Triglycerides	80 mg/100 ml	67 mg/100 ml	+19.4%
Calcium	10.0 mg/dl	9.8 mg/dl	+2.0%
Pi	3.5 mg/dl	3.1 mg/dl	+12.9%
Total Bili.	0.5 mg/dl	0.6 mg/dl	−16.7%
Direct Bili.	0.1 mg/dl	0.2 mg/dl	−50%
Bun/Creat.	14.3	12.5	+14.4%
Sodium	145 mg/liter	138 mg/liter	+5.0%
Globulin	2.3 gm/dl	2.6 gm/dl	−11.5%
Potassium	4.4 meq/liter	4.7 meq/liter	−6.3%
CO_2	25 meq/liter	27 meq/liter	−7.4%
Alkaline Phosphatase	48 u/liter	45 u/liter	+6.6%

AVERAGE % OF VARIATION: 13.5%
(of 16 tests)

The third method scientists use to approach the Cytotoxic test's reproducibility is to draw a tube of blood from a subject on one day and then retest him in a week or a month, or even six months. These scientists contend that the results should be the same in all tests. But no blood test will show the same results after a time lapse. We have found that a person's fixed, major sensitivities will keep appearing, but there are many variables that could make these foods disappear from test results or that could make new ones appear.

One variable is the frequency and quantity of ingestion of the particular food substance. When a food has been totally eliminated from the diet, for example, for more than 280 days (the half-life of the T cells that our research shows carry the codes of the food sensitivity), there are 50 percent fewer cells that can identify the food as foreign and theoretically a substantially lower chance of a sensitivity reaction. After 560 days of total elimination, another 50 percent loss of coded T cells will occur. The longer the food is eliminated, the fewer coded T cells will remain in the body to identify the particular food substance as foreign.

We all have other, nonfixed food sensitivities, and these are always changing, depending on our current eating habits. As an example, supposing I take a Cytotoxic test on a Monday morning, and that afternoon a friend introduces me to some new food I'd never eaten before—say Limburger cheese. I fall in love with the Limburger and eat it twice a day for the rest of the week. If I were to take another test that next Monday, chances are fairly good that the Limburger, or at least some of its ingredients, would show up as sensitivities.

The flaw in Cytotoxic testing is not in its methodology at all. I believe the flaw is in our expectations of the findings. How can we ignore the thousands of variables that exist in the human body during the period of several days', weeks', or months' time?

We expect, because we have been taught to believe, that medicine is a fixed science that can accurately determine our ailments and prescribe remedies for them. This is a false notion in every sense. Medicine is actually as much an art form as a science, and those doctors who look at their profession in that light do the best jobs of helping their patients get well.

One of the reasons nutritional approaches to medical questions are difficult for some medical doctors and scientists to comprehend is that they require less scientific evaluation and more open-minded exploration. The Cytotoxic test gives us a way to begin our investigations. It doesn't hand down a lifetime of rules to follow or even a black and white picture of our problems. It simply gives us a way to begin monitoring our own bodies.

When we eliminate the foods that show up on the Cytotoxic test, or through the other methods outlined in Chapter 9, we begin the process of recovery. But only when science accepts the variables in the human body, its environment, and its stress levels when judging the validity of new medical approaches will there be an end to the question of reproducibility.

Contention #4:
THERE ARE TOO MANY FALSE POSITIVES AND NEGATIVES IN CYTOTOXIC TEST RESULTS

False positives mean that some of the foods that show up as reactive on the Cytotoxic test will not produce visible symptoms when eaten by the person tested. False negatives describe a sensitivity or allergy that the person knows he has but that doesn't show up on the test. Some false positives and negatives can, of course, be blamed on the subjectivity of the testing procedure. Most accusations of false positives, though, show a lack of understanding of what the Cytotoxic effect is all about. If I have a food sensitivity to wheat, for instance, and I eat a slice of bread, I may not show any visible or noticeable symptoms for hours, even days. The symptoms can be so masked that they are not apparent to me. This does not mean that a reaction isn't taking place in my body. My immune system is still being attacked by the food substance, and my allergic threshold is lowered, so that if a virus or infection comes my way, I may be more susceptible to it.

In the case of false negatives, some people expect to see reactions to their known allergens. But, as we have seen, the Cytotoxic test will not isolate an allergy unless it is combined with a Cytotoxic effect, which is often the case. There are blood tests, like the RAST test, that effectively isolate food allergies.

Contention #5:
THE CYTOTOXIC ELIMINATION DIET IS DANGEROUS

The third phase of the Food Sensitivity Diet, as outlined in Chapter 9, is the elimination of all foods to which a person is sensitive. This elimination makes some doctors and nutritionists uncomfortable, because they feel that by avoiding certain nutritious foods for any given amount of time, a state of malnutrition may ensue.

We know that the human body can exist for weeks without any food at all before it shows signs of malnutrition, but our elimination program still leaves plenty of foods in the diet. With all the foods available to us today, the elimination of those that are toxic to our bodies should not cause any loss of nutrition. Some doctors who work with us do prescribe vitamin and mineral supplements for their patients during the elimination phase, especially because some of these supplements help ease withdrawal symptoms and speed the recovery process. A nutritionist or nutritionally oriented physician can easily help with substitute foods and nutritional supplements, if any are needed.

Contention # 6:
SO WHAT IF
A WHITE BLOOD CELL DIES?

The significance of the white cell death we see under our microscopes during the Cytotoxic test is not yet fully understood. Doctors argue that blood cells are born and die all the time. How do we know that foods are causing the neutrophils to explode on the test slide? The control slide provides an answer to this question. For every Cytotoxic test performed, there is a control slide made, which has no food substances inoculated onto it. This control is used as a monitoring device by the technician. If there are white cells dying on the control, the technician knows there is an infection present in the body, and he notifies the referring physician as to the discrepancy.

Under healthy conditions, there will be no cell death apparent on the control slide. As soon as the cells are inoculated onto the other 186 food slides, the technician observes that white cells are exploding on some slides. He will continually monitor the control slide as he reads the others.

We watch the foods assaulting the immune system during the Cytotoxic test. And while we may have only some good scientific guesses at this time as to why a Cytotoxic reaction occurs, we have the best reason in the world to believe in the Cytotoxic effect. People who eliminate the foods that react on their tests feel better. Empirical proof! What more of a reason do we need to believe in the concept?

AN INVITATION

We don't have all the answers yet, but it's exciting and gratifying to know that some of the most qualified and respected research scientists and medical doctors are now interested in Cytotoxic research.

I personally invite qualified health care professionals with a research motivation to contact our staff, make use of our research results, consult with our Ph.D.'s, conduct studies, and use our facilities. Whatever resources are available to me I will make available to them as much as possible. This commitment reflects my genuine interest in furthering research on the Cytotoxic effect.

ONE STUDY

Many studies, scientific and observational, have been conducted by our research team and by others connected with the developing field of Cytotoxic technology. But the one I'd like to describe in detail was conducted by Dr. C. Keith Conners, one of the nation's foremost research scientists. We chose to include his study for two reasons. First, I don't know Dr. Conners, although I have certainly heard of his work. As far as I know, he has no vested interest in Cytotoxic technology. In fact, we came upon his Cytotoxic study by accident, as we were gathering information for our chapter on childhood diseases. His book, *Food Additives for Hyperactive Children*, includes his studies on the subject of Cytotoxic testing.

Second, we use the Conners study because he has an impeccable reputation as a scientist and researcher. A clinical psychologist, he did his postgraduate studies at Oxford on a Rhodes scholarship. He is presently Director of Research at the Laboratory of Behavioral Medicine, Department of Psychiatry, at Children's Hospital in Washington, D.C. He is also one of only about six hundred outstanding scientists who are members of the National Academy of Science.

The Cytotoxic test and its credibility came to Dr. Conners's attention when he was searching for a reliable test to diagnose food allergies in conjunction with his work on food additives and hyperactive children. The skin scratch test, he writes in his book, has not proven reliable, although it is still widely used by allergists, in conjunction with food diaries, elimination trials, and history taking, to construct allergy-free and sensitivity-free diets. He writes:

> The procedure is fraught with problems. It requires complete cooperation by the patient and careful monitoring of the diet. What the patient does and what he reports may not be identical. The problem with children would appear to be even more complicated. It is for these reasons that attempts have been made to develop objective criteria for food allergies such as the RAST test and a method which we decided to investigate called the Cytotoxic test.

With the objective of determining the reliability of the test, Conners sent a technician to Dr. William T. K. Bryan and Marian Bryan, originators of the technique, to learn how to read the slides. He then performed the Cytotoxic test on ninety-five adults and children with behavior problems. He reports:

> All testing was double-blind by the technician who did not know whether the subjects were patients or whether they had suspected allergies. They were tested on at least two occasions, separated by one to three month intervals. Sixty-four foods and nine FD & C colors were tested.

Generally, behavioral scientists would accept a correlation of .70 or greater as satisfactory reliability, though for individual patient diagnosis a reliability of .80 or better is preferred. . . . The overall test-retest reliabilities of the Cytotoxic test were found to be .85, based on those food items in which there were sufficient reactions to calculate a correlation.

In other words, the scientists were pleased with the reproducibility of the test.

This first column of The Conners Study shows the foods used in the test; the second column, the number of people who tested each food on both tests. The third column shows the number of people who showed positive reactions on both tests; the fourth column, the number of people who showed no reaction to the food on both tests. The fifth column shows the number of people who showed different reactions to the food on each test; the sixth column illustrates the reproducibility of the test by listing the correlation between the first and second tests. A correlation of 1.00 equals 100 percent reliability. The overall test-retest reliabilities of the Cytotoxic test, as illustrated by this study, were found to be .85.

Conners's book also cites a small, double-blind study performed by an allergist on thirteen patients to assess the validity of the Cytotoxic test. Conners explains:

He used small capsules of freeze-dried foods and challenged the patients with either a food to which they were known to be allergic, on the basis of the Cytotoxic test, or with a food to which they were not allergic. The patients took the food capsules double-blind over a four-week period. Ten of the patients (all adults) took the capsules according to the prescribed schedule. Nine of these ten showed a positive allergic response to the "active" but not to the control capsules. Only two of the nine reactors had an inconsistent reaction during some weeks and not others. These preliminary results give some confidence that the test may be useful in diagnosis and for constructing elimination diets for treatment.

Cytotoxic Test-Retest Results: The Conners Study

Food Tested	Number of people tested	Reacted on test I and II	No reaction on test I and II	Split	Correlation
Eggs	94	14	70	10	.89
Hops	48	1	46	1	—
Coffee	91	5	78	9	.79
Onions	58	5	52	1	—
Yellow #6	72	2	66	4	.83
Spinach	47	4	41	2	.96
Sugar beets	46	2	44	0	1.00
Bananas	46	2	43	1	—
Blue #1	72	4	65	3	.94
Lettuce	55	0	51	4	—
Wheat	90	9	68	13	.76
Peppermint	48	3	45	0	1.00
Cottonseed	48	1	45	2	—
Strawberries	78	2	67	9	.54
Mustard	48	1	46	1	—
Horseradish	49	0	47	2	—
Oranges	60	1	51	8	.50
Pork	94	9	75	10	.83
Carp	53	2	50	1	—
Milk	93	24	58	11	.92
Sugarcane	83	6	71	6	.89
Barley	48	0	47	1	—
Rice	48	0	48	0	—
Mushrooms	52	5	43	4	.90
Lobster	51	1	45	5	—
Peas	48	0	45	3	—
Peanuts	59	7	49	3	.96
Red #3	56	1	54	1	—
Apples	56	1	54	1	—
Carrots	48	1	45	2	.82
Peaches	48	0	46	2	—
Tuna	57	4	52	1	—
Red #4	59	2	54	3	.86
Soybeans	57	0	52	5	—
Honeydew	51	1	46	4	.66
Chicken	59	3	54	2	.95

Cytotoxic Test-Retest Results: The Conners Study
(continued)

Food Tested	Number of people tested	Reacted on test I and II	No reaction on test I and II	Split	Correlation
Chocolate	92	9	71	12	.78
Beef	59	2	55	2	—
Pears	50	2	47	1	—
White potatoes	58	2	54	2	.91
Turkey	50	0	48	2	—
Pineapple	49	1	46	2	.82
Green #3	74	1	71	2	—
Cantaloupe	46	0	46	0	—
Cherries	46	0	46	0	—
Brewers' yeast	46	0	46	0	—
Shrimp	76	7	61	8	.83
Malt	73	3	68	2	.95
Broccoli	48	0	47	1	—
Trout	49	2	45	2	—
Tobacco	53	5	44	4	—
Tomatoes	89	15	65	9	.91
Rye	49	0	47	2	—
Swordfish	48	0	47	1	—
Orange B	55	1	51	3	—
Bakers' yeast	88	15	62	11	.88
Vanilla	47	0	46	1	—
Garlic	46	0	46	0	—
Crab	46	1	43	2	.81
Kidney beans	48	2	44	2	.91
Watermelon	48	1	45	2	.82
Lamb	48	1	46	1	—
Cucumber	50	3	46	1	—
Blue #2	72	1	69	2	—
String beans	49	0	47	2	—
Veal	50	4	45	1	—
Corn	92	9	72	11	.82
Radishes	46	0	43	3	—
Oats	48	2	45	1	—
Cabbage	48	1	46	1	—
Red #40	62	0	60	2	—
Yellow #5	48	0	46	2	—
Cheese	38	0	38	0	—

In summarizing his Cytotoxic studies, Conners states:

> We have investigated a promising method of detecting food allergies, the Cytotoxic test. We have performed this test on over 300 adults and children, many on two separate occasions. The test appears to be quite reliable. A small, double-blind challenge study showed that in patients with known allergies, the Cytotoxic test predicts to which foods they will show allergic response. Although the validity data are preliminary, they are sufficient to conclude for the moment that the Cytotoxic test is both reliable and valid.

Dr. Conners and his colleagues have performed other studies on the Cytotoxic test and were sufficiently impressed to continue gathering statistics and information.

WHAT YOU SHOULD ASK

I would like to emphasize that while the Cytotoxic test offers the first simple and relatively inexpensive way to isolate food sensitivities, the test itself is only as valid as the expertise of the technician who interprets the reactions. Unfortunately, like many other new medical procedures, there are unqualified people offering the test at this time.

People who seek out innovative products and services are usually keen on making informed decisions for themselves and are able to discern good from bad, capable professionals from impostors. When considering the services of a Cytotoxic laboratory, there are questions you can and should ask to assure yourself that the test is being performed adequately and that you are getting your money's worth. This is extremely important, since at this writing, there are no governing standards set up to monitor Cytotoxic laboratories.

Don't hesitate to inquire as to the training of the laboratory owner and ask for a tour of his facility. If he says he's a doctor, ask to see his license. Here are some questions you may wish to pose when interviewing a Cytotoxic laboratory:

1. How are your technicians trained? The technicians at Physicians Laboratories of California all have extensive science backgrounds. A great majority of them have been personally trained by Dr. T. K. Bryan and Marian Bryan, the pioneers of the Cytotoxic test, at their training laboratory at Washington University School of Medicine in St. Louis. Before our technicians are left on their own to read test results, they spend many months working under the direct supervision of our technical supervisors.

We continually monitor the technicians' competency and accuracy through internal quality control and double-blind tests. At times we will give two technicians samples of blood from the same person, labeled with different names. We will then examine their test results, which should be nearly identical. At other times, we'll give the same technician two samples of blood from the same person again labeled with different names, to see if his test results duplicate, as they should.

These may seem like elaborate procedures, and they are; but our reputation hinges on the accuracy of our tests.

2. What do you charge per food tested? If you are paying more than $1.50 per food tested, you are probably being overcharged. Most Cytotoxic laboratories will include 150 to 200 foods on an average test. Be wary of laboratories offering "special panels" that carry additional charges, like panels for drugs or other exotic substances. The Cytotoxic test observes food sensitivities, and we are not yet sure about its validity when it comes to drug or other environmental, chemical or alcohol reactions. Also, as noted in previous chapters, most alcohol addiction is not to the alcohol itself but to the grains or other ingredients contained in a person's favorite drinks. Grains are tested on the normal Cytotoxic test, as are yeasts, grapes, malt, hops—basically anything that would go into an alcoholic beverage, except the ethyl alcohol. Different drugs react in different ways on the body's various systems. Lack of a Cytotoxic reaction does not necessarily mean that a particular drug is not harmful to your other body systems.

3. What kind of follow-up or diet counseling do you offer? If you don't get some sort of individualized follow-up based on your test results, you won't really be able to make the most of your Cytotoxic test. Some laboratories will offer a class in the evening attended by twenty or so clients who have taken Cytotoxic tests. The laboratory owner, an employee, or doctor will spend a few hours answering questions and explaining the test results. Sometimes he'll pass out a preprinted pamphlet recapping what he said. We don't feel this is adequate follow-up. Some laboratories will give you a rotary, diversified diet plan, either a pamphlet that explains how you can set up your diet or, hopefully, an individualized rotary diet created specifically for you from your test results.

After many years of upgraded service, Physicians Laboratories of California prepares a computer-generated printout, created for each client according to his test results. The first pages of the food program detail a master shopping list of allowable foods for your particular diet. This is a list of all the tested foods that were found to be compatible with your system. The next page is a menu plan for the first day of your four-day rotary diet. It can be kept at home to aid you in preparing meals. On the following page, an alphabetized list of that day's allowable foods is provided, so you can take it with you as a daily shopping list or as a guide to lunch suggestions if you will be away from home. The diet plan for the other three days follows. This takes literally *all* the guesswork out of instituting a Food Sensitivity Diet System into your daily life.

4. How many medical doctors refer patients to you? Do you have a qualified research-and-development department?

Hundreds of medical doctors from across the United States refer patients or send their patients' blood samples to Physicians Laboratories of California for processing. While a majority of physicians are as yet unaware of the Cytotoxic food sensitivity test, we actively pursue and follow up with any medical doctor who desires information on food sensitivities. Our staff of Ph.D's and technicians is always at their disposal. Only in this way will established medicine become aware of the role that food sensitivities play in our overall health and in the disease process.

If the laboratory you are considering appears to be doing an adequate job, let them do your test for you. If not, thanks to recent technological advances, blood samples can be mailed, so even if there is no Cytotoxic laboratory near you, your doctor can draw your blood sample and mail it to a reputable laboratory.

8

Serious Illness

*People have asked what I thought when I was told
by the specialists that my disease was progressive
and incurable.
The answer was simple. Since I didn't accept the
verdict, I wasn't trapped in the cycle of fear,
depression, and panic that frequently accompanies
a supposedly incurable illness. I must not make it
seem, however, that I was unmindful of the
seriousness of the problem or that I was in a
festive mood throughout. Being unable to move my
body was all the evidence I needed that the
specialists were dealing with real concerns. But
deep down, I knew I had a good chance and
relished the idea of bucking the odds.*

NORMAN COUSINS
Anatomy of an Illness

I am afraid that living in a world so full of pollutants, toxins,
and overburdening stresses I or someone in my family will one
day fall victim to cancer, diabetes, an immuno-deficiency disease, or any one of the scores of degenerative or infectious illnesses around us.

Yet, living in fear of these diseases is something I simply refuse to do. As debilitating and frightening as they are, they are often nothing more than out-of-control food or chemical sensitivities.

Most of these diseases are illness cycles that have been building and responding to toxic stimuli for years. To the people who have them, these diseases are grave and life threatening. I only wish they had known to take their symptoms seriously years ago, before the cycles became entrenched and overpowering. Why didn't someone tell the crippled arthritic, for instance, to do something about his symptoms before they became debilitating, when he felt only a slight numbing in his arm or pain in his fingers? So often we and our doctors casually dismiss our headaches, backaches, and sinus problems. Our symptoms are considered everyday by-products of life, nothing to worry about.

Cytotoxic and food allergy research is pointing out that these early symptoms are crucial and their causes should be found if we are to avoid becoming helplessly enmeshed in disease spirals. The body is never frivolous when it signals distress. Its symptoms, however mild, once they start occurring on any kind of regular basis, all mean *something*. Very often that something is the existence of food sensitivities or other toxic reactions that are keeping the body's immune system weakened and are attacking and causing swelling and inflammation of the tissues and organs.

If you are suffering from a serious illness and Cytotoxic testing shows reactions to certain foods, then elimination of these foods may make your symptoms at least feel lighter, easier to bear. This is because a tremendous load is lifted from your immune system. While you've been fighting your disease with only half an immune army, you'll now have most of your defensive force available to you where you need it most.

We often hear people with degenerative diseases report that after isolating and eliminating their food sensitivities, their symptoms don't seem to be getting worse. This means they have halted or at least slowed the deterioration, and their diseases aren't progressing. To someone on the brink of incapacitation, this is quite a blessing.

The link between sensitivity reactions and serious illness is a most recent discovery. We are only beginning to discover the magnitude of the Cytotoxic effect in relation to disease cycles.

Beginning with very early man and continuing right through the eighteenth century, infectious diseases took turns playing havoc with the earth's human population. In the fourteenth century, for example, the bubonic plague killed off a third of Europe's population. It's difficult to imagine the horrendous scope and magnitude of these rampaging epidemics and the helplessness people must have felt in facing them.

The Industrial Revolution ushered in the beginning of the end of the great epidemics, although the early 1900s certainly had their share of influenza and other viral attacks. But great strides were soon made in conquering infectious diseases, and today we no longer live in fear of an epidemic racing through our cities and towns. Tuberculosis, which was at one time responsible for about 20 percent of all deaths in Western countries, is almost nonexistent today. Measles, which once affected nearly everyone, has become almost extinct, thanks to anti-measle inoculations. Cases of whooping cough have come down from 250,000 patients in 1939 to 2,000 cases in 1982. In the 1920s, there were 200,000 cases of diphtheria; today there are fewer than 100 cases a year. (These figures are from *Maximum Life Span* by Roy L. Walford, M.D.)

In this century, some of the great accomplishments made by modern medicine have been in the area of trauma injury; we now see dynamic medical teams in ultramodern hospital emergency rooms handle even the most horrendous accident traumas swiftly and expediently. They perform what would have been considered miracles even a short decade ago.

Computer technology has taken much of the guesswork out of many medical testing procedures, and computers have literally taken over the monitoring of critically ill patients in hospitals. New microsurgery techniques allow orthopedic surgeons to perform joint surgeries using tiny television cameras attached to the ends of fiber-optic scopes, which they insert into the joint. The camera allows the surgeon to see and record whatever is going wrong in the joint, while a probe, manipulated by the surgeon from outside the patient's body, performs the surgery. No surgical incision is required, only a small puncture wound that heals easily.

These are only a few of thousands of examples we could cite that illustrate how far medical technology has come in recent years. But there is one type of human malady that continues to dodge the very best efforts of modern medical research: the degenerative diseases. These are the diseases of our own making. By overindulging in the wrong foods, by polluting our air and water, and by living in constant emotional stress, we have created a new generation of illness.

It is said that there are some 100 different types of cancer and almost as many variations of arthritis in existence today, to say nothing of the nerve-degenerating diseases like multiple sclerosis, amyotropic lateral sclerosis, Parkinson's disease, and the rest. The rise in the number of reported cases of lupus, celiac disease, diabetes, gout, hypoglycemia, anorexia/bulimia, and the many other gruesome names that have become all too familiar to us today point out, in no uncertain terms, our victimization by the very things we have created. More and more research points out that the causes of these illnesses are, indeed, man made.

The degenerative diseases are frustrating because they seem unflappable in their resistance to medical technology. True, we have developed elaborate treatments for the symptoms of some of these illnesses, like chemotherapy, radiation therapy, surgery; but in treating the symptoms of degeneration, we often compound the problem or create side effects that are as bad, if not worse, than the disease itself.

We are beginning to question our medical approaches, and with good reason. We must rethink the issue and examine our unyielding devotion to drug therapy and symptomatic relief. We must also take a look at our expectations of our medical professionals, because when it comes to degenerative diseases, no one has the answers. It seems incredible to consider, even for a minute, that degenerative diseases are often rooted in abused food sensitivities. But they well might be.

There are many thousands of people who have brought about their own remissions from degenerative diseases. When we hear their stories, we shake our heads in wonderment. They may inspire in us a hope that either faith in God or a positive attitude or maybe even vitamins are the answer.

While we do tend to underestimate the curative powers of

faith, attitude, and nutrients, we must also realize that when we see a remission from a disease, we are not witnessing a miracle or observing a simple answer. We are seeing the results of dedication and hard work in the face of almost impossible odds.

Famed playwright Roger MacDougall, a multiple sclerotic who successfully fought his disease and won, has had his diagnosis of MS questioned many times by puzzled and disbelieving doctors. He was first diagnosed as having the disease in 1953 by a leading London physician. MS is characterized by a progressive deterioration from which no one supposedly returns, and he was given, at the most, five years to live. MacDougall found himself confined to a wheelchair, unable to move his fingers or toes, nearly blind, hardly able to speak.

In 1975, twenty-two years after his original diagnosis, he visited the doctor who had diagnosed his MS and requested a complete neurological work-up. The doctor found that every muscle, every reflex, every movement was perfectly normal. The only trace of MacDougall's MS was a slight juddering of the optic nerve, which affects only the farthest extremity of his field of vision as he glances to the right. This same nystagmus was so bad at one time that he was at the point of virtual blindness. What transpired during twenty-two years between his original diagnosis and his hearing the astounded doctor pronounce him "all clear" proved to be a learning experience that is now benefiting many thousands of MS sufferers. MacDougall cured himself by isolating and eliminating his food sensitivities.

He is now positive that foods are the underlying cause of his multiple sclerosis, a disease which also afflicted his mother, his mother's brother, and another uncle. MS, he says, is his family's "Achilles' heel." Even though Roger MacDougall believed he was genetically predisposed to MS, he did not accept the hopelessness of his condition. Here, in part, is his own story, as related in his booklet, *My Fight against Multiple Sclerosis:*

> I have no medical training. I was, however, trained in logic after taking a law degree at Glasgow University, and this training was of considerable help to me in developing my approach.
> Logic told me that, since multiple sclerosis was ap-

parently caused by the breakdown of the myelin sheath surrounding the nerves, it was likely to be a degenerative condition.

I also suspected that multiple sclerosis was as much a biochemical problem as a medical one. More specifically, I assumed that multiple sclerosis was caused by a chemical imbalance resulting in the inability of the body to create replacement tissue for the myelin layer surrounding the nerves.

In other words I came to regard the body as a chemical process and multiple sclerosis as a manifestation of that chemical process going wrong.

These suppositions led me to believe that multiple sclerosis might be controlled by adjusting the food intake in a way which would correct the offending chemical imbalance.

I therefore decided that I should pursue the approaches which were medically accepted as helpful in the treatment of other degenerative conditions. These were:

A gluten-free diet, which removes the symptoms of coeliac disease.

A sugar-free diet, which is indicated in cases of diabetes and hypoglycaemia.

A diet free of milk-fat, which appears to help those with cardiovascular conditions.

Over the course of the next few years, I dropped the suspect foods from my diet one after another. At first I merely stabilized the state of my symptoms; then, slowly and steadily, my health improved. Slowly is the word I must emphasize. It was more than four years before I noticed the first significant improvement when I managed to fumble a shirt-sleeve button into a button-hole—the first time my fingers had obeyed a command in a very long time.

Thus encouraged, I took a closer interest in the problem of nutrition in relation to my condition.

Over the years, I refined my dietary recommendations in the light of my own experiences and other people's.

Roger MacDougall carved out his "logical" diet and somehow managed to isolate and eliminate his major food sensitivities.

Working only on instinct and logic, he was able to guess at the correct ones.

Years later, after he had put his MS into remission, Roger visited Physicians Laboratories of California and took the Cytotoxic test. It confirmed the accuracy of his eliminations across the board and added a few foods he had never thought about. In a letter to *Let's Live* magazine, he wrote:

> I was first introduced by Doug Kaufmann to the increasingly popular Cytotoxic test at a laboratory in the Los Angeles area.
>
> The results of my test were significant to me for two reasons. They showed why I had recovered from MS. I had identified my major allergies—grains (gluten), milk products, sugar, oranges, tomatoes, tobacco. They also identified a few other allergies of which I had not been aware, particularly onions, rice, corn and apples . . . This Cytotoxic test which proved so accurate in my case seems to me superior in almost every respect to any of the other tests.

MacDougall, now fully mobile, spends most of his time in correspondence with thousands of MS sufferers, many of whom follow his dietary regimen of isolating and eliminating their food sensitivities. He reports many, many success stories.

Links between degenerative diseases and the Cytotoxic effect can be seen through their mutual impact on the white blood cells. In a paper entitled "Cancer and Your Diet," dated March 1977, Nathan Pritikin recounts an experiment performed by a German doctor, Otto Warburg, in which he put cells in bell jars and lowered the amount of oxygen in the jar below atmospheric concentration. He began to notice that the cells started to "get sick. They would move around lazily. Some would even change their structure." He found that if he lowered the atmospheric pressure 60 percent or more below normal, a number of the cells would die and others would survive, but change their structure and begin to look like malignant cancer cells. He found he could produce malignant characteristics in as little as forty-eight hours by depriving the cells of sufficient oxygen.

Other researchers continued Dr. Warburg's work and found

that they could produce malignant growths by taking normal cells transformed by a lack of oxygen and injecting them into animals.

Lack of oxygen in the cells can be a direct result of the Cytotoxic effect. We have seen that the edema caused in the food sensitivity reaction is often responsible for cutting off oxygen to blood vessels supplying the body's organs. Since research has shown that oxygen-deprived cells can easily become malignant, isn't it natural to inquire as to the correlation between food sensitivities and cancer?

Applying what Cytotoxic research proves by way of our nutritional individuality, it seems that there are as many degenerative diseases as there are people in the world. Each and every one of us is suffering from some kind of degeneration. This degenerative side of you becomes evident when the "domino theory" takes over; the cold sore you had last spring turned into gum disease, which caused, after a while, swollen glands and a sore throat with high temperature. You never consciously connected these symptoms, except to note that some little thing or another has been bothering you constantly for the past year or so. This is the beginning of a degenerative chain, and if its progress is not halted, it will climb to new plateaus of illness. The immune system is being constantly bombarded, weakened. What happens when it gets so far out of hand that medicine can't help?

How do you know when you have the beginnings of a degenerative disease? There are no medical tests that will tell you if you've got a degeneration going on in your body. You may notice, though, that your headaches are coming twice a day now, instead of just a few times a week, as they had been for years. Now both arms hurt instead of just one. Your lower back pain comes on more intensely and more often. You find yourself needing medicine for one thing or another more often, and trips to the doctor are more frequent. You have less willpower and find yourself more and more attracted to addictive foods, beverages, and chemicals. Your self-observation should be approached with more logic than emotion. Logic will help you connect seemingly unrelated symptoms to a degenerative process and will keep you from denying your symptoms.

If you're healthy now, consider yourself lucky, because if you start avoiding toxins now, you may head off the serious degeneration that might come on later. Think about it; the foods you are eating now may be contributing to your future health problems. All those delicious things you love to eat may be slowly killing you.

In an article in *Let's Live* magazine, Roger MacDougall writes: "It's a strange paradox; by overindulgence, by pleasing his fancy; man slowly poisons himself in a way that is so slow-acting that the casual connection has never been seen and is indeed stoutly denied by people who should know better." His message holds true; overindulgence is the key to degenerative cycles.

A CASE OF ANOREXIA

The list of newly documented degenerative diseases is growing by leaps and bounds. It's possible, of course, that they have always been around, but were never before recognized. Anorexia nervosa and its close cousins, bulimia and bulimarexia, affecting mostly women and young girls, are good examples of newly labeled degenerative disorders whose numbers seem to be growing dramatically each year. Statistically, the diseases affect upper-middle-class white girls, generally the type who want only to please, who get good grades in school, and who are competitive by nature.

The following case history of anorexia/bulimia took place almost fifteen years ago, when the disease was barely recognized and when only a few people knew anything about the Cytotoxic test.

Jill was a sixteen-year-old high-school student, a quiet girl who got good grades in school and who was always eager to please her teachers, family, and friends. Her best friend announced one day that she was starting a weight-loss diet, which was the "in" thing to do. Jill didn't understand her friend's wanting to diet, as she had a nice figure and never complained about being fat. But her competitive drive took over, and soon Jill began a diet of her own. She noticed that she lost weight easily and felt a sense of accomplishment. The competitive situation between the two girls started snowballing, and before long, Jill, at 5'8", weighed 88 pounds—and she still felt fat.

Delusions about fatness are typical of the anorexic, as are their covert eating habits. Jill recalls that she took over her family's shopping, cooking, and meal planning, just so she could have control over the food they had in the house and the meals that would get prepared. She and her girl friend, who also became anorexic, would trade recipes and discuss food; their relationship became totally centered around their mutual obsession with eating. Jill's most comfortable meals were taken in private; she hated to eat when other people were watching.

On a typical morning, Jill would eat only a tiny breakfast. She would have no food at all during school hours. After school, she would head straight home, intensely hungry, and proceed to binge on all her craved-for sweets and baked goods, as well as any other food she could get her hands on. An anorexic/bulimic can swallow, in one sitting, a couple of family-size bags of cookies, followed by a few bowls of cereal, some bagels smothered with butter, washed down by two or three cups of coffee or glasses of milk. Some chocolate bars and a bag of pretzels later, she will force herself to throw up all the food she's just eaten. During this process, she'll get on and off the scale to see if she's gained any weight.

In Jill's case, this binge-purge cycle went on every day for three years. Like most anorexics, she stopped menstruating, and she had what she now looks back on as an unconscious desire to remain childlike, to avoid having to live up to the ridiculous standards society sets up for womanhood. The thinness of high fashion models and actresses, the perfection of their bodies, is an unattainable goal that a girl who is naturally competitive might strive toward.

But while psychiatrists have thrust the entire question of anorexia into the realm of emotional disorder, in more and more cases we are finding that food sensitivities are a central part of the process.

Jill's parents rejected the idea of psychotherapy for their daughter, and instead requested that a Cytotoxic test be done on her. Her test showed a high reaction to sugar and reactions also to bakers' yeast and milk. Sugar, she recalls, was her favorite thing—sweets are what she would crave the most, and baked products with yeast and milk products like ice cream were close runners-up.

When she eliminated these foods and the others that showed up on her test results, she gained ten pounds in the first month and a half. Her weight slowly came back, the vomiting addiction was broken, and her menses returned. The whole process took about two years. Now she can eat most of the sensitive foods, as long as she doesn't overdo.

Jill's is an isolated case, but one that is typical of her condition. She leads us to the logical conclusion that what we need to be concerned with in the anorexic is not what isn't being eaten, which is what we normally think about when someone is ingesting only 300 to 600 calories a day, but what remains in the diet. The anorexic's body signals provide a graphic call for help. Losing her desire to eat, her adrenalin flows, creating a mood of intense hatred for food. She is obsessed with the kinds of foods that are being bought, prepared, and eaten; and she displays an emaciated, underweight appearance. She eats and then vomits. How much more of a distress call could the body possibly send out that what is being ingested is also being rejected, in every way?

I'm sure the next decade will reveal, scientifically, the links we see existing between many types of degeneration and the Cytotoxic effect. It's only a matter of time before we unravel the mysterious processes that cause diseases like leukemia, a cancer of the white blood cells, where we see a tremendous rise and then a dangerous drop in the white blood cell count that never comes back to normal. Frightening diseases like sudden infant death syndrome, Legionnaires Disease, or the acquired immunodeficiency syndrome (AIDS)—which is spreading so rapidly—may be just more variations on the same theme. Medical research hopes that by studying the diseases' effects, it will discover their causes. I believe this approach will only continue treating symptoms and never touch the causes.

As Roger MacDougall writes in *Let's Live* magazine: "The medical study of effects has swamped the entire area of the degenerative conditions with a mass of research into the irrelevant." His MS, named after the symptoms his illness displayed, would be far more aptly named if it had been called "Sugar-wheat-dairy-itis."

It's interesting to note that both Jill and Roger had the same fixed sensitivities, yet their symptoms were as varied as they could possibly be.

CANDIDA ALBICANS— BECOMING ALLERGIC TO YOURSELF

There is one group of people my heart really goes out to, because even though theirs is a most serious physical illness, they are virtually ignored, discredited, and even ridiculed by the medical establishment and by the world in general. These people are teetering on the brink of total immunological collapse. They are sensitive or allergic to almost everything they eat and come in contact with. They are considered "weird" by friends and family, and they receive little, if any, help from doctors or drugs. We find them needlessly relegated to mental institutions or sitting alone at home, unable to do even the most basic things. They are more than likely to think of themselves as "mental cases" because no one has a clue as to what's bothering them.

An inroad has recently been made, though, into one possible cause and cure of this syndrome. A handful of medical doctors are now studying the effects of a kind of yeast infection, called Candida albicans, that is often responsible for this severe sensitivity illness. If there is a Candida condition present, isolating and eliminating food sensitivities will not bring the needed results. If Candida is suspected, it should be discussed with a nutritionally oriented physician who can prescribe the proper treatment.

Candida albicans is a yeast. Yeasts are organisms, like fungal molds. Molds are everywhere, in the soil, they grow on surfaces of materials containing organic components. The air is filled with mold spores. Other molds live on the surface of and within animals, including humans. Candida albicans is a mold that normally exists in human beings in the skin or vagina.

Many women, especially if they take birth control pills or contraceptive hormones, experience what are called yeast infections. These infections don't mean there is a serious Candida problem existing in the rest of the body, but they do signal the potential of the yeast spreading to other organs.

Antibiotics, especially broad-spectrum antibiotics that kill many of the bacteria normally present in the intestinal tract and in the vagina, also cause the spread of the Candida. These bacteria retard yeast growth, and when they are destroyed, there is often a flare up and swift spread of the Candida yeast.

Candida is often present in newborn babies from the first day of life. This is no problem when the body's bacteria keep the Candida to a low level, but often young babies will get a Candida infection following an encounter with antibiotics, which are prescribed freely to babies who show signs of croup, colds, ear infections, bronchitis, etc.

In adults, the danger of the Candida infestation is that in a few people it will travel from the cavities of the intestine or vagina and penetrate and grow in the tissues of the body. It is then able to release its fungal products into the bloodstream, where it travels from organ to organ, causing inflammation, edema, and constant attack on the immune system. When this happens, the body has actually become sensitive, or allergic, to itself, and the resulting symptoms can be devastating.

The growth of Candida is stimulated by certain elements of people's diets, like carbohydrates—starches and sugars. Proteins and fats are less well utilized by the fungi. Foods with their own high content of yeast or mold can cause an increase in allergic symptoms, especially fermented beverages, wine and beer, aged cheeses, mushrooms, vinegar, and breads with a lot of yeast.

If a case of supersensitivity exists that doesn't respond to the elimination of Cytotoxically sensitive foods (see Chapter 9), we suggest investigating the possibility of a Candida condition being present in the body.

AGING: A DISEASE?

We have entered, as Roy L. Walford, M.D., describes it, the Age of Degenerative and Man-made Diseases. When we conquer the problem of degeneration—heart disease, cancer, diabetes, arthritis, and the rest—will the process of aging also be cured? Is aging a disease? I think not, but I do think that disease need not be an inevitable part of the aging process.

Because it fears death, our culture takes all the joy out of the aging process. People over sixty-five tend to be abused by every other group in our society, including the people they depend on the most, their doctors. Medicine is full of big words that mean very little to the lay person, and this is especially true in gerontology. If you're over sixty-five, your doctor is probably telling you to expect some of your systems to start breaking down: your senses, especially hearing and eyesight, will become weaker and weaker, your memory will start going, and your physical acumen will slowly deteriorate. I say this is poppycock!

If you're sixty-five, and you've spent the last fifty-five years of your life eating foods to which your body is sensitive, then you may expect your hearing or eyesight or any other bodily function to start deteriorating. This is a kind of degeneration. Fifty-five years of stress is a lot for any body to bear. But if you remove these toxic foods from your diet, your body will respond with healthy cells and a stronger immune system. Your doctor may tell you that your symptoms are "normal," but you need to consult with the "doctor" inside you. You may be experiencing difficulty getting up in the morning, bad digestion, constipation, joint pain—but is the person inside really feeling "old"? Perhaps you are placing too much credence in aging and its supposed symptoms and not enough in the abuse you may unknowingly be doing to your body every day through food sensitivity.

It's a good idea to keep in touch with your doctor. Your body has been serving you for sixty-five years or more, and you should be giving it the best care. But the truth is that your body will live as long as its cells live. Keeping the cells thriving in old age may take more attention than it did when you were younger. The years of stress do create a lowered threshold. But your cells will respond when oxygenated by exercise, when fed foods that don't cause toxic response, and when they are provided with a full range of nutrients.

Many old people have started saying "goodbye" to their bodies, and this is unfortunate. During this phase of life, a little vanity, a bit of self-absorption and self-nurturing is the best prescription in the world.

There's no reason for the aging process to be riddled with disease, discomfort, illness. My feeling is that these are caused, at any age, by the same factors. The problem with aging is not in the aging process, but in our expectations that this phase of our life must be accompanied by a set of degenerative symptoms.

Our research so far points out, in no uncertain terms, that aging can be an easy winding down of life's many involvements, a peaceful time of reflecting on and enjoying the wisdom gathered from years of living.

PART II

THE
FOOD
SENSITIVITY
DIET

CUSTOMIZED UNIQUELY
FOR EACH INDIVIDUAL

9

The
Phases of the Diet

*. . . Man's strongest desires are not for health,
but for life and living . . . Health is not an
end in itself, but a means of attaining life's
purposes. So while we may conclude that
health concerns do not deserve our
preoccupation, we do need to occupy
ourselves with them to help assure the
attainment of life's goals.*
J. S. SINACORE
Health: A Quality of Life

Anyone can live a fuller, healthier, more enjoyable life by applying the Food Sensitivity Diet System. Even if you don't experience more than an occasional headache or viral attack,
you'll be amazed at the difference in your life when you eliminate toxic foods.

More than twenty thousand people have taken Cytotoxic
tests at our laboratories, and not one person has ever come out
completely free of food sensitivities. We all have them, even
top athletes who spend most of their time perfecting their bodies and looking after their health. Food sensitivities keep us *all*
from performing at our optimum level.

I've had many people tell me things like, "You know, I thought I was fairly intelligent, sharp, and quick witted all my life. But after following a Food Sensitivity Diet, I feel as if I've been in a fog for the past thirty years. I've never experienced such clarity of thought before!" Someone else said, "I had become so accustomed to all those little aches and pains, my irritability after work, the two or three colds a year and that constant battle with about five pounds of extra weight. I guess I just sort of incorporated them into my life and worked around them. Now they're gone, and in their absence, I realize how under the weather I really was all the time."

People with obvious symptoms, of course, have a great deal of incentive to get going and begin their recovery. The main thing to remember is that when you begin changing eating habits you've been cultivating for a lifetime, things can get tricky, no matter how much you may want to get rid of your painful symptoms. Some of us find it difficult to break the emotional ties we have for certain foods—especially if we connect them with the nurturing love of our childhoods. I can only say, the love affair just ain't worth it!

One of the most important things to remember is that this is not a permanent diet. Basically, once the offending foods are removed from the diet, the body soon regains its strength. In the long run, there may be a few foods that will always bother you, but you will be able to eat some quantities of all the rest.

The Food Sensitivity Diet progresses through four phases, which vary in length of time according to your individual degree of sensitivity. The four phases are as follows:

I   Determination
II   Isolating the Sensitivities
III Eliminating the Sensitive Foods
IV   Challenging and Reintroduction

PHASE I: DETERMINATION

The first step in the Food Sensitivity Diet System is putting yourself into the right frame of mind. The diet will not only make you healthier; the real rewards are that your body and mind will be more finely tuned than ever before, allowing you to enjoy life to the fullest.

So, set your mind on the type of life you would like to be living, the type of person you know you are when not overburdened by feelings of exhaustion, ill health, and mental fuzziness. Think about the proper weight for yourself. Are there dreams, ambitions that are beginning to seem too difficult or maybe even impossible at this stage of your life? You'll be amazed at what you can accomplish when you're feeling good, so set your sights high!

The beauty of the Food Sensitivity Diet is that it brings you and your body into focus as partners in the healing process. When you take a Cytotoxic test or use one of the other testing methods outlined in the chapter, your body tells you which food substances are hampering its smooth operation, and you do whatever it takes to avoid these substances.

Your body responds by offering more energy, clearer thought processes, more access to creative channels. This makes it easier to stick to the diet. If you get sloppy, especially during the first few weeks, your body will let you know it in no uncertain terms by producing vivid symptoms. A partnership in health!

Understanding and utilizing Cytotoxic technology is a personal thing, even if you are being guided through the process by a physician or nutritionist. The set of foods you eliminate is unique to you, as are your needs for additional vitamins and minerals, the length of time you will need to stay away from certain foods, and most of all, the way you go about including the plan in your day-to-day life.

Everyone deals with this in a different way, and the Food Sensitivity Diet is flexible enough to let you do what's right for you. Some people find it easier to ease into the diet, eliminating one or two things at a time until they have excluded them all. This approach doesn't work for other people, who seem to do best going "cold turkey" on all their sensitivities from the onset. The Food Sensitivity Diet, as you will see, can be adapted to your particular needs and abilities. Go slowly, listen to your body, and you'll soon discover the path that's right for you.

FOOD WITHDRAWALS

The thought of having withdrawal symptoms from eliminating bananas from your diet or developing unbearable cravings for a slice of bread may be difficult to take seriously. But, for some people, eliminating a food that has been a main staple of their diet for years can and does cause some discomfort. Consider these signals your first sign that the diet is working (see Chapter 5).

Some people find themselves feeling shaky or enduring headaches for a few days after taking certain foods out of their diets. Disorientation is another common withdrawal reaction. Often, people are convinced that withdrawal symptoms are "all in the mind." They're not—they are distinct physical signs that you are clearing your body of its sensitivities.

Though the withdrawals you may feel during the initial absence of a food to which your body has become addicted can sometimes be profound, they usually don't last more than a few days, or a week at the most. Sometimes it's helpful to ease yourself off the sensitive foods, eliminating them gradually over a period of days or even weeks. When you consider that foods, like drugs, are chemical combinations that react on many of the body's organs and systems—including the nervous system—it's easier to understand the food withdrawal process.

With these things in mind, you're now ready to find out which foods are giving you problems.

PHASE II: ISOLATING THE SENSITIVITIES

THE CYTOTOXIC TEST

By far, the easiest way to isolate food sensitivities is by taking the Cytotoxic test. This test requires a small blood sample to be drawn from your arm. The blood sample is laboratory-prepared and then placed on slides. Each of your slides is preinoculated with a different food substance and then placed under a microscope and observed by a technician. The technician can observe some of these food substances killing your white blood cells on the slides, and these are considered foods to which your body is sensitive.

Physicians Laboratories of California tests 186 food substances on each blood sample. Why 186 foods? First of all, many of the foods we eat, like mayonnaise or bologna, are actually combinations of several foods, so our 186-food roster represents a broad spectrum of basic foods. Also, the more foods we test, the wider the variety of foods you'll be able to eat on your Food Sensitivity Diet. For instance, if you're sensitive to 30 out of 186 foods, it will be much easier to create a livable diet than it would be if you reacted to 30 out of only 50 foods tested. There wouldn't be much left to eat!

About twenty-four hours after taking the Cytotoxic test, your results come back on a form that lists the 186 foods tested, broken down into fifty "food families." Food families are groups of foods that are organically similar.

The test results show damage to your blood cells measured on a scale of 1 to 4 reactions. A #1 reaction indicates that the food caused platelet aggregation. Platelets are colorless discs circulating in the blood that aid in clotting. They are also valuable to many other processes, like helping to keep the walls of the blood vessels clean of debris. When the foods we eat continually cause the platelets to clump together, they are not available to perform their functions adequately.

A #2 reaction indicates that the food has caused a slight damage to the white blood cells; a #3 reaction indicates that the food has caused moderate damage to the white blood cells; a #4 reaction shows severe damage to the white blood cells and some damage to the red blood cells as well. This 1–4 scale is a comparative ratio, but doesn't necessarily correlate to the severity of the symptoms that may be produced.

SAMPLE CYTOTOXIC TEST RESULTS

Reactions are noted on a scale of 1 to 4 reactions. Foods tested are broken down into food families.

REACTION	1	2	3	4	FOODS
					Banana
1	☐	☐	☐	☐	banana
					Beech
2	☐	☐	☐	☐	chestnuts
					Bellflower, Thistle
3	☐	☐	☐	☐	artichoke
4	☐	■	☐	☐	lettuce
5	☐	☐	☐	☐	safflower oil
6	☐	☐	☐	☐	sunflower oil
					Berch
7	☐	☐	☐	☐	filbert
					Brassica
8	☐	☐	☐	☐	broccoli
9	☐	☐	■	☐	Brussels sprouts
10	☐	☐	☐	☐	cabbage
11	☐	■	☐	☐	cauliflower
12	☐	☐	☐	☐	kale
13	☐	☐	☐	☐	radish
14	☐	☐	☐	☐	turnip
					Buckthorn
15	☐	■	☐	☐	grape, raisin
					Buckwheat
16	☐	☐	☐	☐	buckwheat
17	☐	☐	☐	☐	rhubarb
					Carica
18	☐	☐	☐	☐	papaya
					Carrot
19	☐	☐	☐	☐	caraway
20	☐	☐	☐	☐	carrot
21	■	☐	☐	☐	celery
22	☐	☐	☐	☐	parsnip

REACTION	1	2	3	4	FOODS
					Cashew
23	☐	☐	☐	☐	cashew
24	☐	☐	☐	☐	mango
					Cereal Grains (grasses)
25	☐	☐	■	☐	barley
26	☐	☐	☐	☐	cane sugar
27	☐	☐	☐	■	corn (maize)
28	☐	■	☐	☐	corn gluten
29	☐	☐	☐	☐	corn sugar
30	☐	■	☐	☐	hops
31	☐	☐	☐	☐	malt
32	☐	☐	☐	☐	millet
33	☐	☐	■	☐	oats
34	☐	☐	☐	☐	rice
35	☐	☐	☐	☐	wild rice
36	☐	☐	☐	☐	rye
37	☐	☐	■	☐	wheat
					Composite
38	☐	☐	☐	☐	endive
					Cyperaceae
39	☐	☐	☐	☐	water chestnuts
					Bony Fish
40	☐	☐	☐	☐	bass
41	☐	☐	☐	☐	catfish
42	☐	☐	☐	☐	cod
43	☐	■	☐	☐	flounder
44	☐	☐	☐	☐	halibut
45	☐	☐	☐	☐	herring
46	☐	☐	☐	☐	mackerel
47	☐	☐	☐	☐	mullet
48	■	☐	☐	☐	perch

REACTION	1	2	3	4	FOODS
					Bony Fish
49	■	□	□	□	red snapper
50	□	□	■	□	salmon
51	□	□	□	□	sardine
52	□	□	□	□	smelt
53	□	□	□	□	sole
54	□	□	□	□	swordfish
55	□	□	□	□	trout
56	□	□	□	□	tuna
					Cartilaginous Fish
57	□	□	□	□	shark
					Crustaceans
58	□	□	□	□	crab
59	□	□	■	□	lobster
60	□	□	□	□	shrimp
					Farinosa
61	□	□	□	□	pineapple
					Fungus
62	□	□	□	□	bakers' yeast
63	□	□	■	□	brewers' yeast
64	□	□	□	□	mushroom
					Ginger
65	□	□	□	□	ginger
66	□	□	□	□	turmeric
					Gourd Order
67	□	□	□	□	cantaloupe
68	□	□	□	□	Cranshaw melon
69	■	□	□	□	cucumber
70	□	□	□	□	honeydew melon
71	□	□	□	□	pumpkin
72	□	□	□	□	squash (summer)
73	□	□	□	□	squash (winter)
74	□	□	□	□	watermelon
					Heath
75	□	□	□	□	blueberry
76	□	□	□	□	boysenberry
77	□	□	■	□	gooseberry

REACTION	1	2	3	4	FOODS
					Honeysuckle
78	□	□	□	□	cranberry
					Laurel
79	□	■	□	□	avocado
80	□	□	□	□	cinnamon
					Legume
81	■	□	□	□	alfalfa
82	□	□	□	□	bean (kidney)
83	□	□	□	□	bean (lima)
84	□	□	□	□	bean (mung)
85	□	□	□	□	bean (pinto)
86	□	□	□	□	bean (soy)
87	□	□	■	□	bean (string)
88	□	□	□	□	black-eyed pea
89	□	□	□	□	carob
90	□	□	□	□	chickpea (garbanzo)
91	■	□	□	□	lentil
92	□	□	□	□	pea
93	□	□	□	□	peanut
94	□	□	□	□	split pea
					Lily
95	□	□	□	□	asparagus
96	□	□	□	□	chives
97	□	□	□	■	garlic
98	□	□	□	□	leek
99	■	□	□	□	onion
					Madder
100	□	□	□	□	coffee
					Mulberry
101	□	□	□	□	fig
					Mallow
102	□	□	□	□	cottonseed
					Mammals
103	□	□	□	□	beef
104	□	□	□	□	butter
105	□	□	□	□	calf's liver
106	□	□	□	□	cheese (American)

REACTION	FOODS

	1 2 3 4	**Mammals**
107	□ □ □ □	cheese (blue)
108	□ ■ □ □	cheese (cottage)
109	□ □ □ □	cheese (mozzarella)
110	□ □ □ □	cheese (Parmesan)
111	□ □ □ □	cheese (provolone)
112	□ □ □ □	cheese (Swiss)
113	□ □ ■ □	cow's milk
114	□ □ □ □	lamb
115	□ □ □ ■	pork
116	□ □ □ □	yogurt
		Maple
117	□ □ □ □	maple sugar
		Mollusks
118	□ □ □ □	abalone
119	□ □ □ □	clam
120	□ □ □ □	oyster
		Mustard
121	□ □ □ □	collard greens
122	□ □ □ □	mustard
		Myristiceae
123	□ □ □ □	nutmeg (mace)
		Myrtle
124	□ □ □ □	clove
		Nightshade
125	□ □ □ □	eggplant
126	□ □ □ □	paprika
127	□ □ □ □	chili pepper
128	□ □ □ □	garden peppers
129	□ □ □ □	potato
130	□ □ □ □	tobacco
131	□ ■ □ □	tomato
		Nightshade-Mint
132	□ □ □ □	peppermint (spearmint)
133	□ □ □ □	sage
		Nightshade-Morning Glory
134	□ □ ■ □	sweet potato (maroon) yam
135	□ □ □ □	sweet potato (yellow)

REACTION	FOODS

	1 2 3 4	**Nightshade-Pedalium**
136	□ □ □ □	sesame
		Orchid
137	□ □ □ □	vanilla
		Palm
138	□ □ □ □	date
139	□ □ □ □	coconut
		Parsley
140	□ □ □ □	watercress
		Pepper
141	□ □ □ □	black pepper
		Pink
142	□ □ □ □	beet
143	□ □ □ □	beet sugar
144	□ □ □ □	spinach
145	□ □ □ □	Swiss chard
		Poultry
146	□ □ □ □	chicken
147	□ ■ □ □	chicken egg white
148	□ □ ■ □	chicken egg yolk
149	□ □ □ □	duck
150	□ □ □ □	goose
151	□ □ □ □	pheasant
152	□ □ □ □	turkey
		Rose
153	□ □ □ □	apple
154	□ □ □ □	apricot
155	□ □ □ □	blackberry
156	□ □ □ □	cherry (prunus)
157	□ □ □ □	nectarine
158	□ □ □ □	peach
159	□ □ □ □	pear
160	□ □ □ □	plum, prune
161	□ ■ □ □	strawberry
		Rue
162	□ □ □ □	grapefruit
163	□ □ □ □	lemon
164	□ □ □ □	lime

REACTION	FOODS	REACTION	FOODS
1 2 3 4	**Rue**	**1 2 3 4**	**Other**
165 ☐☐☐☐	orange	175 ☐☐☐☐	allspice
166 ☐☐☐☐	tangerine	176 ☐☐☐☐	almond
	Sapucaia	177 ☐☐☐☐	food coloring
167 ☐☐☐☐	Brazil nut	178 ☐☐☐☐	goat's milk
	Spurgel	179 ☐☐☐☐	honey
168 ☐☐☐☐	curry	180 ☐☐☐☐	horseradish
169 ☐☐☐☐	tapioca, cassava, yucca	181 ☐☐☐■	MSG
	Sterculia	182 ☐☐☐☐	olives
170 ☐☐☐■	cocoa, chocolate	183 ☐☐☐☐	oregano
171 ☐☐☐☐	cola nut	184 ☐☐☐☐	saccharin
	Tea	185 ☐☐☐☐	thyme
172 ☐☐☐☐	tea, black		
	Walnut		
173 ☐☐☐☐	pecan		
174 ☐☐☐☐	walnut		

IF YOU CAN'T TAKE A CYTOTOXIC TEST

If you have no access to the Cytotoxic test, you can still isolate many of your sensitivities. It takes a little work, but it will be well worth the effort. One way to begin is to refer to the chart below, which lists the "Top 50" food sensitivities that show up when we compare results of our Cytotoxic tests. For example, you can see that about 45 percent of the tests show reactions to coffee and 36 percent to onions.

Think about these foods in relation to your own diet. If you find that you eat any one of them every day, or even every other day, there's a good chance that you have a sensitivity/addiction cycle at work with that food. Try eliminating the substance from your diet for a week. If there is an addiction, you will probably experience some physical discomfort or withdrawal symptoms (see Chapter 5), like headaches or heavy cravings for the food.

Top Fifty Food Sensitivities

(Tallied from Cytotoxic test results at Physicians Laboratories of California)

Food	Percent of Tests Showing Reactions
Cow's milk	58.6%
Wheat	54.9%
Coffee	45.1%
Brewers' yeast	44.3%
Cottage cheese	38.4%
Corn	38%
Potato	37.3%
Onions	36.5%
Cane sugar	35.4%
Butter	34.9%
Peanuts	34.9%
Blue cheese	34.6%
Corn gluten	34.6%
Rye	34.6%
Bakers' yeast	33.2%
Beef	33.2%
Tobacco	33.2%
Parmesan cheese	32.7%
Buckwheat	31.1%
American cheese	30.8%
Almonds	30.5%
Cocoa/chocolate	30.0%
Tuna	30.0%
Sunflower oil	29.7%
Soybean	29.7%
Grapes	29.5%
Pork	29.2%
Monosodium glutamate (MSG)	28.4%
Yogurt	28.1%
Cola nut	27.8%
Garlic	27.6%
Leeks	26.5%

Swiss cheese	26.2%
Tea	26.2%
Tomato	25.4%
Chili pepper	24.6%
Shrimp	24.6%
Cinnamon	24.1%
Chicken	23.5%
Paprika	23.5%
Provolone cheese	23.5%
Strawberries	23.2%
Corn sugar	22.9%
Mushrooms	22.7%
Oranges	22.7%
Broccoli	22.4%
Hops	21.6%
Black pepper	21.1%
Mozzarella cheese	20.8%
Oats	20.8%

THE DIET DIARY

To further help isolate your individual sensitivities, keep a diet diary. Follow the instructions carefully, and keep track of everything you eat during an average one-week period. Don't change any of your normal eating habits. Any food that appears more than three or four times a week is suspect as a sensitivity, although you probably are not sensitive to *all* the foods you eat often.

People who have very routine diets, who eat basically the same foods every day, may have a difficult time with the initial elimination phase of the diet, for they are the ones who often turn out to be sensitive to everything they eat. If you fall into this category, you will be doing yourself a great favor by changing and adding variation to your diet. Overuse or abuse of foods is a major cause of food sensitivity.

It is critically important that the information you record in your diet diary be as accurate and complete as is humanly possible. The relationship between what you choose to eat and

EXAMPLE OF A CORRECTLY FILLED OUT DIARY PAGE

If you follow the rules, your diary will look something like the following example. These entries are, of course, imaginary and not intended to suggest menus for you to follow.

SAMPLE DIET DIARY

TIME	FOOD-DRINK-MEDICATIONS	TIME	SYMPTOMS (0-4)
		12:00–7:30	Up twice during night with coughing and sneezing
7:30	Awakened		No symptoms
8:15	Orange juice, unsweetened Wheaties, sugar, milk, English muffin/butter, apple jelly, Coffee, cane sugar, cream		
		9:30	Runny nose-2+ sneezing-2+
		10:00	No symptoms
		12:00	No symptoms
12:30	Vegetable soup (beef stock, peas, carrots, celery, potatoes) Ham sandwich, whole wheat bread, butter, mustard White cake-chocolate icing Coffee, sugar, cream		
		1:00	Trouble breathing-4+ Felt faint-lasted 10 minutes
3:00	Glass of milk		
		3:10	Stomach pains-4+
3:15	2 antacid tablets		
		3:30	No symptoms
		5:45	Stuffy nose-1+
6:30	Dry martini		
7:15	Tomato juice, fried chicken, peas, mashed potatoes, butter Salad-lettuce, tomato, carrots, pepper, artichoke, blue-cheese dressing Vanilla ice cream, chocolate sauce		
		8:00	Belching-1+ Nausea-2+
8:15	2 antacid tablets		
10:00	Glass of milk	10:30	Hives on neck for one hour-4+
11:30	Went to bed		

your symptoms may be very simple or very complex. For example, some foods may give a delayed reaction many hours after you eat them. Others may cause an immediate discomfort. Still other foods may cause more evident symptoms on some days than on others.

1. Write down everything you ingest, including water, medicines, vitamins, snacks, alcoholic beverages, soft drinks, cigarettes.

2. List the composition of mixed dishes and combinations of foods. It is not enough to write down "a ham sandwich." You should also indicate the kind of bread, spread, and dressing (ham sandwich, whole wheat bread, butter, mustard). Whenever you make an entry in your diary, ask yourself if you've given yourself enough information.

3. List all your symptoms and always indicate exactly when the symptoms started, how long they lasted, and how severe they were. To assist you in identifying the symptoms, refer to the chart of Common Symptoms of Food Sensitivities on pp. 110–111.

4. Don't put off filling out the diary until the end of the day or before you go to sleep at night. Fill out the information just after eating. Memory is often unreliable. It's a good idea to carry the diary with you during the day.

5. List your symptoms on a basis of 0 to 4, which indicates their severity.

6. Be sure to record an observation of your symptoms before each meal or snack and again 30 to 60 minutes afterward.

THE FASTING/FOOD-CHALLENGE REGIMEN FOR DETERMINING FOOD SENSITIVITIES

The chart showing the most common food sensitivities on pp. 110–111 will give you some clues as to what your individual food incompatibilities may be. The diet diary will bring you even closer to isolating your particular set of sensitivities. But to really be sure, without taking the Cytotoxic test, many food-sensitivity specialists put their patients on a fasting/food-challenge regimen.

First, you must fast (water only) for four days. We have observed that it takes about four days for food substances to clear out of the digestive system. Avoid everything, even vitamins, during the fast, because vitamins often contain binders and excipients made of corn, soybean, yeast, or other substances that elicit a high percentage of intolerance.

If you are taking any kind of medication, you should, of course, work closely with a nutritionally oriented doctor during the fast. Fasting can be very therapeutic, especially to a food sensitive person. As the toxins leave your body during the food fast, you may experience a surprising feeling of exuberance. It's not unusual for me to get a call from someone on his third day of a fast, telling me he's feeling fantastic. While we expect to feel terrible without food, the opposite is often the case, because energy that normally goes into fighting the toxic foods is now available to energize the body.

Don't worry, you won't starve during a four-day fast. In fact, Allan Cott, M.D., author of *Fasting: A Way of Life,* says: "The body has in reserve at least a month's supply of food. It nourishes itself during a fast as if it were continuing to receive food."

Any headaches, tiredness, or other symptoms you may experience while fasting are probably food addiction/withdrawal symptoms, rather than weakness from not eating food. Occasionally, though, these symptoms will signal a hypoglycemic (or other medical) condition. As opposed to the food sensitive person, the hypoglycemic may not feel better while fasting. Instead, he may develop heavier symptoms. If your symptoms persist or worsen after two or three days of fasting, a medical doctor should be consulted.

After the fourth day of fasting, you are ready to give yourself some food "challenges" to determine sensitivity. Consult your diet diary and choose a food you eat most often, perhaps carrots. Eat a plain carrot (it's crucial to test only one food substance at a time). Monitor yourself for reactions. An incompatible food is identified by the body as "foreign" as soon as it hits the mucous membrane under the tongue. After a fast, if there is to be a reaction to the food, it will usually happen quickly and will be rather noticeable. Sometimes there are exceptions and symptoms will be delayed, occurring as long as twelve to twenty-four hours after ingestion. If your sinuses clog up, if a headache or stomach ache develops, if your eyes start feeling puffy or watery, or if you begin to feel dizzy or angry— anything unusual or uncomfortable—there is a reaction going on. After an hour or so, "challenge" another food, and monitor yourself for reactions. This fasting/food-challenge regimen is time consuming, but it can help isolate food sensitivities when the Cytotoxic test isn't available.

Some reactions, of course, have nothing to do with food sensitivities. If you down a cup of coffee after a five-day fast, chances are you'll notice a real "high" as soon as the caffeine hits your system. Sugar substances may react in the same way, even if no sensitivity exists. So common sense should prevail.

PHASE III: ELIMINATION

Once you determine the foods to which you may be sensitive, either through Cytotoxic testing, by referring to the percentage chart, by keeping a food diary, or by using the fasting/food-challenge regimen, you are now ready to start the elimination phase of the Food Sensitivity Diet. Make a list of your food sensitivities and keep it with you at all times. You will need to eliminate them from your diet completely.

There is a wide variation in the way each individual clears his system of food sensitivities. Your personal reactions depend on many factors, including, but not limited to, the severity of the sensitivity, your emotional ability to stick to the elimination diet, and the foods to which you may have developed addictions. As a rule of thumb, reactive foods should be totally eliminated for at least two months, for this seems to be the length of time required to "clear" most sensitivities. Some people, though, take much longer and others may take only a few weeks before they can start reintroducing foods into their diets.

After working with thousands of people who eliminated toxic foods, I have observed a general pattern that most of us follow. The first few days of elimination of intolerant foods are the most difficult, especially the second day. It's as if the immune system wakes up on the second morning and suddenly realizes there won't be that toxic stimulation it has grown to expect for any number of years. It panics and calls out massive immune attacks, as it would normally do when toxic foods are ingested. But there's nothing for these white cells to attack. The results are withdrawal symptoms and sometimes extreme food cravings, *not to be confused with hunger.*

I like to suggest that people begin the elimination program at a time of relatively low stress—start it on a Friday, for example, so you can have the weekend to rest. Even if you don't experience withdrawal symptoms during this period, your body is still going through a shocking sequence of events, and a few days' rest will help it cope.

Symptoms usually wear off after the first four days of elimination, and then many people begin to experience a feeling of energy, strength, and well-being. It's crucial at this point to be very careful to avoid all foods that may contain substances you wish to eliminate. Sometimes, even a small amount may be enough to trigger a reaction or to keep the sensitivity active. Remember to read all labels on packaged foods carefully. If your symptoms don't disappear in a few days, and there's no hypoglycemic condition, it's possible that one or two of these foods are still being eaten. Even a tiny amount of some substances can keep the immune system attacking and the sensitivity reaction active, so much care should be taken.

The next seven or eight weeks of elimination, for some people, is a period of supersensitization. If they accidentally eat one of their intolerant foods during this time, their symptoms *may* come back more severely than before. If wheat, for example, tended to produce headaches or dizziness under old dietary conditions, then eating it after a week or two of elimination might bring on migraines. Not everyone experiences this severity of symptom response and not all sensitive foods will bring it on in those who do become "supersensitive." Close monitoring of all body signals is the best way to judge how rigid your elimination diet should be.

ROTATION

During Phase III, it's important to rotate carefully the rest of the foods you are eating. Rotating foods means not eating the same food more than once every four days. This will keep you from building up new sensitivities that can result from overusing any of the foods you may eat.

If you are eliminating eggs, for example, and start eating oatmeal every morning for breakfast instead, your chances of becoming sensitive to oats are great. Instead, have oatmeal one morning, sweetened with honey. Next morning, try Cream of Rice cereal sweetened with maple syrup, and the next day try a baked yam for a real change of pace.

For help rotating your diet, consult the sample rotary diets appearing in the next chapter. There are also sources that will supply you with computerized rotary diets, created from your individual list of food sensitivities.

PHASE IV: CHALLENGE AND REINTRODUCTION

Our Cytotoxic research has shown us that of the average twenty-five or thirty foods that show up as sensitivities on the Cytotoxic test, only two or three, if any, will have to be permanently eliminated from the diet. The others become problems only when overconsumed.

After the two-month elimination period, it's time to start reintroducing foods in a slow, systematic "food challenge" program.

It's important to institute these food challenges one at a time, keeping a food diary and writing down any symptoms that might appear. Don't trust your memory! Do you remember what you ate for lunch two days ago? I imagine not!

FOOD COMBINING FOR EASIER DIGESTION

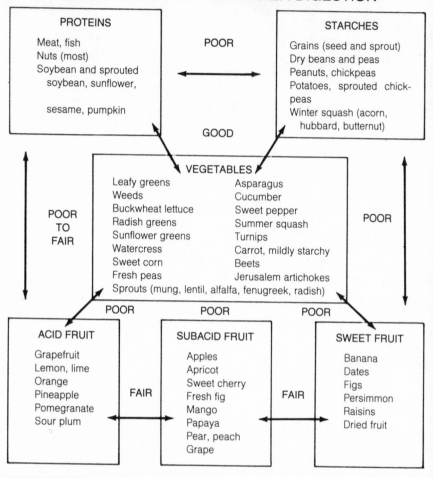

PROTEINS	STARCHES

Meat, fish
Nuts (most)
Soybean and sprouted
   soybean, sunflower,
 	
   sesame, pumpkin
	Grains (seed and sprout)
	Dry beans and peas
	Peanuts, chickpeas
	Potatoes, sprouted chick-
	   peas
	Winter squash (acorn,
	   hubbard, butternut)

POOR

GOOD

VEGETABLES

Leafy greens	Asparagus
Weeds	Cucumber
Buckwheat lettuce	Sweet pepper
Radish greens	Summer squash
Sunflower greens	Turnips
Watercress	Carrot, mildly starchy
Sweet corn	Beets
Fresh peas	Jerusalem artichokes

Sprouts (mung, lentil, alfalfa, fenugreek, radish)

POOR TO FAIR

POOR

POOR   POOR   POOR

ACID FRUIT	SUBACID FRUIT	SWEET FRUIT
Grapefruit Lemon, lime Orange Pineapple Pomegranate Sour plum	Apples Apricot Sweet cherry Fresh fig Mango Papaya Pear, peach Grape	Banana Dates Figs Persimmon Raisins Dried fruit

FAIR   FAIR

GOOD COMBINATIONS

Protein and leafy greens
Starch and vegetables
Oil and leafy greens
Oil and acid fruit
Oil and subacid fruit

POOR COMBINATIONS

Protein and acid fruit
Leafy greens and acid fruit
Leafy greens and subacid fruit

BAD COMBINATIONS

Protein and starch
Oil and protein
Starch and fruit

From "Love Your Body" by Viktoras Kulvinskas M.S.

To challenge a food, make "mono-meals" of only one food out of the Cytotoxically reactive foods. This is important because you won't get a clear reading of your reactions if two or more Cytotoxically reactive foods are mixed at any one meal. If you are sensitive to potatoes but not to butter, you may have a potato with butter on it. But if you are also reactive to sour cream, don't add it.

Be sure to challenge each reactive food at least three days apart and at least twice. Meanwhile, stick to your normal diet, continuing to eliminate the unchallenged foods and rotating the rest. If there is no reaction, you may incorporate the challenged food back into your diet on a rotating basis. Just write it down on any day's plan. As you challenge and reintroduce sensitive foods, be aware of the reappearance of any symptoms and write them into your food diary.

COMBINING FOODS

There are certain foods that seem to combine well on a universal basis, although we have learned that nothing in nutrition is truly universal. As a rule of thumb, though, consult the food-combining chart below. Meat and potatoes are a classically poor food combination, while meat and leafy green vegetables seem compatible. If you are rotating your diet and feel you have isolated and eliminated most of your food sensitivities, you should be symptom free, unless there are other allergies—inhalant, animal danders—or sensitivities that haven't been isolated (many people are sensitive to tap water). There's also a chance that you are having what we call a concomitant reaction due to poor food combining.

10

The Rotary Diet

While you are eliminating sensitive foods from your diet, and even after you have successfully cleared you body of its food sensitivities, it is important to rotate foods that you are eating. As we have said before, rotation prevents new sensitivities from developing—remember that the prime reason sensitivities exist is overexposure to certain foods. Be careful not to eat the same food more than once every four days.

Here is a sample rotary diet, which you can adapt to your own food sensitivity program. Simply replace the foods to which you are sensitive with other foods from the same "food family." The rotary diet is created by including foods from various food families (listed below) on each day's eating plan.

Food Families

Banana
Banana

Beech
Chestnuts

Bellflower, Thistle
Artichoke
Lettuce
Safflower Oil
Sunflower Oil

Berch
Filbert

Bony Fish
Bass
Catfish
Cod
Flounder
Halibut
Herring
Mackerel
Mullet
Perch
Red snapper
Salmon
Sardine
Smelt
Sole
Swordfish
Trout
Tuna

Brassica
Broccoli
Brussels sprouts
Cabbage
Cauliflower

Kale
Radish
Turnip

Buckthorn
Grape, raisin

Buckwheat
Buckwheat
Rhubarb

Carica
Papaya

Carrot
Caraway
Carrot
Celery
Parsnip

Cartilaginous Fish
Shark

Cashew
Cashew
Mango

*Cereal Grains
(Grasses)*
Bamboo shoots
Barley
Cane sugar
Corn (maize)
Corn gluten
Corn sugar
Hops
Malt
Millet
Oats
Rice

Rye
Wheat
Wild rice

Composite
Endive

Crustaceans
Crab
Lobster
Shrimp

Cyperaceae
Water chestnuts

Farinosa
Pineapple

Fungus
Bakers' yeast
Brewers' yeast
Mushroom

Ginger
Ginger
Turmeric

Gourd Order
Cantaloupe
Cranshaw melon
Cucumber
Honeydew melon
Pumpkin
Squash (summer)
Squash (winter)
Watermelon

Heath
Blueberry
Gooseberry

Honeysuckle
Cranberry

Laurel
Avocado
Bay leaf
Cinnamon

Legume
Alfalfa
Bean (kidney)
Bean (lima)
Bean (mung)
Bean (pinto)
Bean (soy)
Bean (string)
Black-eyed pea
Carob
Chickpea (garbanzo)
Lentil
Pea
Peanut
Split pea

Lily
Asparagus
Chives
Garlic
Leek
Onion
Shallot

Madder
Coffee

Mallow
Cottonseed

Mammals
Beef
Butter
Calf's liver

Cheese (American)
Cheese (blue)
Cheese (mozzarella)
Cheese (Parmesan)
Cheese (provolone)
Cheese (Swiss)
Cow's milk
Lamb
Pork
Yogurt

Maple
Maple sugar

Mollusks
Abalone
Clam
Oyster

Mulberry
fig

Mustard
Collard greens
mustard

Myristicaceae
nutmeg (mace)

Myrtle
Clove

Nightshade
Eggplant
Paprika
Chili peppers
Garden peppers
Potato
Tobacco
Tomato

Nightshade-Mint
Peppermint (spearmint
Sage

Nightshade-Morning Glory
Sesame

Orchid
Vanilla

Palm
Date
Coconut

Parsley
Watercress

Pepper
Black pepper

Pink
Beet
Beet sugar
Spinach
Swiss chard

Poultry
Chicken
Chicken, egg white
Chicken, egg yolk
Duck
Goose
Pheasant
Turkey

Rose
Apple
Apricot
Blackberry
Boysenberry
Cherry (*Prunus*)
Nectarine
Peach
Pear
Plum, prune
Strawberry

Rue
Grapefruit
Lemon
Lime
Orange
Tangerine

Sapucaia
Brazil nut

Spurgel
Curry
Tapioca

Cassava
Yucca

Sterculia
Cocoa
Chocolate
Cola nut

Tea
Tea, black

Walnut
Pecan
Walnut

Other
Allspice
Almond
Food coloring
Goat's milk
Honey
Horseradish
MSG
Olives
Oregano
Thyme

FOUR DAY DIVERSIFIED ROTARY DIET

Foods listed on the Four Day Diversified Rotary Diet are broken down by food families and are divided by four days, so no food is eaten more than once every four days. The foods that you are sensitive to should be crossed off the list. You may eat as much as you like of any foods listed for a given day, but only on that day.

DAY NO. 1

Food Group	Food	Food Group	Food
Grains	Barley	Protein	Abalone
	Corn sugar		Blue cheese
	Rice		Chicken
			Cod
Fruits	Apple		Duck
	Blueberry		Halibut
	Coconut		Mackerel
	Gooseberry		Parmesan cheese
	Lemon		Provolone cheese
	Orange		Shark
	Pineapple		Swiss cheese
	Watermelon		Turkey

DAY NO. 1

Food Group	Food	Food Group	Food
Vegetables	Avocado	Other	Bakers' yeast
	Brussels sprouts		Brewers' yeast
	Celery		Chestnuts
	Corn gluten		Cocoa, chocolate
	Fig		Curry
	Kidney bean		Honey
	Lima bean		MSG
	Onion		Oregano
	Pinto bean		Saccharin
	Rhubarb		Sunflower oil
	String bean		
	Turnip		

DAY NO. 2

Food Group	Food	Food Group	Food
Grains	Buckwheat	Protein	American cheese
	Hops		Butter
	Rye		Chicken, egg white
			Cottage cheese
Fruits	Apricot		Flounder
	Boysenberry		Herring
	Cranberry		Mozzarella cheese
	Grape		Perch
	Lime		Red snapper
	Papaya		Shrimp
	Plum/prune		Swordfish
			Yogurt
Vegetables	Alfalfa	Other	Beet sugar
	Beet		Caraway
	Cabbage		Cassava
	Chickpea		Chili peppers
	Cucumber		Coffee
	Garden peppers		Filbert
	Leek		Horseradish
	Yam		Mustard

DAY NO. 2

Food Group	Food	Food Group	Food
	(continued)		
	Parsnip		Paprika
	Potato		Safflower oil
	Spinach		Tapioca
	Summer squash		Vanilla
	Watercress		Yucca

DAY NO. 3

Food Group	Food	Food Group	Food
Grains	Cane sugar	Protein	Bass
	Millet		Calf's liver
	Wheat		Chicken, egg yolk
			Cow's milk
Fruits	Banana		Goat's milk
	Cantaloupe		Lamb
	Cranshaw melon		
	Grapefruit		Mullet
	Mango		Pheasant
	Peach		Salmon
	Strawberry		Smelt
			Trout
Vegetables	Artichoke		
	Black-eyed pea	Other	Allspice
Carrot			Black pepper
	Chives		Carob
	Eggplant		Cinnamon
	Garlic		Cola nut
	Lentil		Food coloring
	Mung bean		Malt
	Pea		Nutmeg
	Pumpkin		Pecan
	Split pea		Sage
	Swiss chard		Tea
	Winter squash		Walnut

DAY NO. 4

Food Group	Food	Food Group	Food
Grains	Corn/maize	Protein	Beef
	Oats		Catfish
	Wild rice		Clam
			Crab
Fruits	Blackberry		Goose
	Cherry		Lobster
	Date		Oyster
	Honeydew		Pork
	melon		Sardine
	Nectarine		Sole
	Pear		Tuna
	Tangerine		
Vegetables	Asparagus	Other	Almond
	Broccoli		Brazil nut
	Cauliflower		Cashew
	Collard greens		Clove
	Endive		Cottonseed
	Kale		Ginger
	Lettuce		Maple sugar
	Mushroom		Olives
	Peanut		Peppermint/
	Radish		spearmint
	Soybean		Sesame
	Tomato		Thyme
	Yellow sweet		Water chestnut
	potato		

Here is a sample of an individualized rotary diet prepared by Physicians Laboratories, Inc., of California. It includes a master shopping list and menus of allowable foods for each day of the four-day cycle. This person had thirty-one sensitivities. The diet that follows excludes his particular intolerances.

ROTATING DIET

Prepared for: BOB R. NEALON   *Date:* 04/13/83

Master List of Sensitivities and Degree of Sensivitity Minimum (1) to Maximum (4)

FOOD	SENSITIVITY
Allspice	2
Artichoke	2
Barley	4
Blackberry	1
Black-eyed pea	4
Blueberry	4
Chestnuts	2
Chicken egg	2
Chives	2
Coconut	4
Cola nut	3
Curry	2
Eggplant	3
Horseradish	2
Kale	3
Lobster	2
Mackeral	2
Mozzarella cheese	1
Monosodium glutamate (MSG)	4
Mullet	1
Nectarine	2
Nutmeg	2
Onion	2
Pecan	2
Plum/Prune	1
Rye	3
Tea	4
Trout	2
Vanilla	4
Walnut	1
Yellow sweet potato	3

THE F.I.T.
(FOOD INCOMPATABILITY TEST)
SYSTEM

Prepared for: BOB R. NEALON   *Date:* 04/13/83
Testing by: PHYSICIANS LABORATORIES, INC., OF CALIFORNIA

ROTATING DIET

Prepared for: Bob R. Nealon   *Date:* 04/13/83

Master Shopping List of Allowable Foods

FOOD

Abalone	Calf's liver
Alfalfa	Cane sugar
Almond	Cantaloupe
American cheese	Caraway
Apple	Carob
Apricot	Carrot
Asparagus	Cashew
Avocado	Catfish
Bakers' yeast	Cauliflower
Banana	Celery
Bass	Cherry (*Prunus*)
Beef	Chicken
Beet	Chicken, egg yolk
Beet sugar	Chickpea (Garbanzos)
Black pepper	Chili peppers
Blue cheese	Cinnamon
Boysenberry	Clam
Brazil nut	Clove
Brewers' yeast	Cocoa/Chocolate
Broccoli	Cod
Brussels sprouts	Coffee
Buckwheat	Collard greens
Butter	Corn/Maize
Cabbage	Corn gluten

Master Shopping List of Allowable Foods

Corn sugar
Cottage cheese
Cottonseed
Cow's milk
Crab
Cranberry
Cranshaw melon
Cucumber
Date
Duck
Endive
Fig
Filbert
Flounder
Garden peppers
Garlic
Ginger
Goat's milk
Goose
Gooseberry
Grape
Grapefruit
Halibut
Herring
Honey
Honeydew melon
Hops
Kidney bean
Lamb
Leek
Lemon
Lentil
Lettuce
Lima bean
Lime
Malt
Mango

Maple sugar
Maroon sweet potato/Yam
Millet
Mung bean
Mushroom
Mustard
Oats
Olives
Orange
Oregano
Oyster
Papaya
Paprika
Parmesan cheese
Parsnip
Pea
Peach
Peanut
Pear
Peppermint/Spearmint
Perch
Pheasant
Pineapple
Pinto bean
Pork
Potato
Provolone cheese
Pumpkin
Radish
Red snapper
Rhubarb
Rice
Safflower oil
Sage
Salmon
Sardine
Sesame

Master Shopping List of Allowable Foods

Shark
Shrimp
Smelt
Sole
Soybean
Spinach
Split pea
Strawberry
Sting bean
Summer squash
Sunflower oil
Swiss chard
Swiss cheese
Swordfish
Tangerine

Tapioca/Cassava/Yucca
Thyme
Tomato
Tuna
Turkey
Turmeric
Turnip
Water chestnut
Watercress
Watermelon
Wheat
Wild rice
Winter squash
Yogurt

ROTATING DIET

Prepared for: BOB R. NEALON   *Date:* 04/13/83

Day 1 Menu of Allowable Foods

FOOD GROUP	FOOD	
Grains	Buckwheat	
	Hops	
	Wheat	
Fruits	Banana	Lime
	Cranberry	Peach
	Grape	Tangerine
Vegetables	Avocado	Parsnip
	Cabbage	Potato
	Chickpea (Garbanzos)	Spinach
	Endive	Summer squash
	Kidney bean	Watercress
	Lima bean	

Day 1 Menu of Allowable Foods

Protein	Bass	Oyster
	Calf's liver	Pork
	Clam	Sardine
	Crab	Sole
	Goose	Turkey
Other	Bakers' yeast	Ginger
	Brewers' yeast	Mustard
	Chili peppers	Peppermint/Spearmint
	Coffee	Sesame

ROTATING DIET

Prepared for: BOB R. NEALON   *Date:* 04/13/83

Day 1 Shopping List of Allowable Foods

FOOD	Avocado	Kidney bean
	Bakers' yeast	Lima bean
	Banana	Lime
	Bass	Mustard
	Brewers' yeast	Oyster
	Buckwheat	Parsnip
	Cabbage	Peach
	Calf's liver	Peppermint/Spearmint
	Chickpea (Garbanzos)	Pork
	Chili peppers	Potato
	Clam	Sardine
	Coffee	Sesame
	Crab	Sole
	Cranberry	Spinach
	Endive	Summer squash
	Ginger	Tangerine
	Goose	Turkey
	Grape	Watercress
	Hops	Wheat

ROTATING DIET

Prepared for: BOB R. NEALON   *Date:* 04/13/83

Day 2 Menu of Allowable Foods

FOOD GROUP	FOOD	
Grains	Cane sugar	
	Millet	
	Wild rice	
Fruits	Boysenberry	Mango
	Cranshaw melon	Pear
	Fig	Watermelon
	Grapefruit	
Vegetables	Beet	Pea
	Carrot	Pumpkin
	Collard greens	Split pea
	Leek	Swiss chard
	Maroon sweet potato/Yam	Winter squash
Protein	Beef	Parmesan cheese
	Catfish	Provolone cheese
	Cod	Shark
	Duck	Swiss cheese
	Halibut	Yogurt
Other	Beet sugar	Olives
	Caraway	Saccharin
	Cinnamon	Sunflower oil
	Cottonseed	Turmeric
	Honey	

ROTATING DIET

Prepared for: BOB R. NEALON   *Date:* 04/13/83

Day 2 Shopping List of Allowable Foods

FOOD

Beef	Mango
Beet	Maroon sweet potato/Yam
Beet sugar	Millet
Boysenberry	Olives
Cane sugar	Parmesan cheese
Caraway	Pea
Carrot	Pear
Catfish	Provolone cheese
Cinnamon	Pumpkin
Cod	Shark
Collard greens	Split pea
Cottonseed	Sunflower oil
Cranshaw melon	Swiss chard
Duck	Swiss cheese
Fig	Turmeric
Grapefruit	Watermelon
Halibut	Wild rice
Honey	Winter squash
Leek	Yogurt

ROTATING DIET

Prepared for: BOB R. NEALON   *Date:* 04/13/83

Day 3 Menu of Allowable Foods

FOOD GROUP	FOOD	
Grains	Corn/Maize	
	Oats	
Fruits	Apple	Honeydew melon
	Cantaloupe	Orange
	Date	Pineapple

Vegetables	Alfalfa	Mung bean
	Broccoli	Peanut
	Cauliflower	Radish
	Corn gluten	Soybean
	Garden peppers	Tomato
	Lentil	

Protein	Abalone	Malt
	Blue cheese	Oregano
	Chicken	Safflower oil
	Cottage cheese	Tapioca/Cassava/Yucca
	Flounder	Water chestnut

Other	Almond	Herring
	Black pepper	Perch
	Carob	Red snapper
	Clove	Shrimp
	Filbert	Swordfish

ROTATING DIET

Prepared for: BOB R. NEALON   *Date:* 04/13/83

Day 3 Shopping List of Allowable Foods

FOOD	Abalone	Corn gluten
	Alfalfa	Cottage cheese
	Almond	Date
	Apple	Filbert
	Black pepper	Flounder
	Blue cheese	Garden peppers
	Broccoli	Herring
	Cantaloupe	Honeydew melon
	Carob	Lentil
	Cauliflower	Malt
	Chicken	Mung bean
	Clove	Oats
	Corn/Maize	Orange

Oregano   Shrimp
Peanut   Soybean
Perch   Swordfish
Pineapple   Tapioca/Cassava/Yucca
Radish   Tomato
Red snapper   Water chestnut
Safflower oil

ROTATING DIET

Prepared for: BOB R. NEALON   *Date:* 04/13/83

Day 4 Menu of Allowable Foods

FOOD GROUP	FOOD	
Grains	Corn sugar	Rice
Fruits	Apricot	Lemon
	Cherry (*Prunus*)	Papaya
	Gooseberry	Strawberry
Vegetables	Asparagus	Mushroom
	Brussels sprouts	Pinto bean
	Celery	Rhubarb
	Cucumber	String bean
	Garlic	Turnip
	Lettuce	
Protein	American cheese	Pheasant
	Butter	Salmon
	Cow's milk	Smelt
	Goat's milk	Tuna
	Lamb	
Other	Brazil nut	Maple sugar
	Cashew	Paprika
	Cocoa/Chocolate	Sage
	Food coloring	Thyme

Prepared for: BOB R. NEALON   *Date:* 04/13/83

Day 4 Shopping List of Allowable Foods

FOOD

American cheese	Lettuce
Apricot	Maple sugar
Asparagus	Mushroom
Brazil nut	Papaya
Brussels sprouts	Paprika
Butter	Pheasant
Cashew	Pinto bean
Celery	Rhubarb
Cherry (*Prunus*)	Rice
Cocoa/Chocolate	Sage
Corn sugar	Salmon
Cow's milk	Smelt
Cucumber	Strawberry
Garlic	String bean
Goat's milk	Thyme
Gooseberry	Tuna
Lamb	Turnip
Lemon	

FOUR-DAY DIVERSIFIED
ROTARY DIET #2
(WITH RECIPES)

This diet presents a complete selection of all food families, rotated on a four-day cycle. No eliminations have been made. To tailor this rotary diet to your own sensitivities, delete those foods to which you are sensitive. You may replace the deleted foods with allowable foods from the same food families.

In this rotary diet, the recipes for each day contain only those ingredients called for on that particular day.

These recipes are designed to be simple, using a minimal array of ingredients. Remember that the purpose of the rotary diet is to avoid repetition in your diet, and simplicity is the key. Juggling too many different foods increases the changes of repetition. When selecting recipes from your own cookbooks to adapt to your food sensitivity diet, stick to the basics and look for recipes that invite substitution of ingredients.

(Provided by Elizabeth Kupsinel, Ann Pasnak and Georgia Kleinhenz, Lost Horizon Health Awareness Center, Shangri-LaLane, P.O. Box 550, Oviedo, Florida 32765. Booklet: "What Can I Eat? Ideas for the Rotary Diet.")

Day No. 1	—Allowable Foods
Buckthorn	Grapes, raisins
Palm	Coconut, coconut oil, date, date sugar
Beech	Chestnut
Pepper	Black and white peper
Lily	Onion, garlic, asparagus, chives, leeks, shallots
Laurel	Avocado, cinnamon, bay leaf
Nightshade	Potato, tomato, eggplant, chili, red and green peppers, paprika, cayenne, capsicum
Poultry	Chicken, turkey, duck, goose, pheasant, eggs
Mammal	Beef, veal, milk, butter, cheese, gelatin
Cereal Grains	Corn, wheat, barley, rye, oats, rice, cane, bamboo shoots, millet
Fungus	Mushrooms, bakers' yeast, brewers' yeast
Honey	Clover honey
Nighshade-mint	Peppermint, mint, spearmint, thyme, marjoram, savory, basil, sage
Other	Oregano

ROTARY DIET DAY NO. 1

Breakfast Ideas

∽ BARLEY PANCAKES

1 cup barley flour
2 teaspoons baking powder
1 egg, beaten

1 cup milk
2 tablespoons corn oil

Combine ingredients; batter should be thin. Bake on hot griddle. Serve with clover honey. Makes 12 pancakes.

Variations: Add raisins or coconut to batter.

∽ RAISIN COCONUT SPREAD

½ cup raisins
½ cup coconut shreds

yogurt

Blend raisins and coconut. Moisten with yogurt. Good for breakfast or in a sandwich. Makes 1 cup.

Salads and Main Dishes

∽ GUACAMOLE SALAD

2 medium avocados, peeled
and cut in small cubes
1 can (14½-ounce) sliced

tomatoes, drained; or 2
medium ripe tomatoes
½ cup diced onion

Combine ingredients well. Serve with Chili Dressing (following recipe). Makes 4 servings.

~ CHILI DRESSING

½ cup corn oil
2 cloves garlic, minced

½ teaspoon clover honey
¾ teaspoon chili powder

Mix ingredients well. Add to guacamole salad, toss lightly, and chill well.

~ CREAM OF AVOCADO SOUP

2 large avocados
1 cup half-and-half

2 cups chicken broth
Sour cream to garnish

Cut the avocados in half. Remove the seeds and scoop out the flesh. Place the avocado flesh and half-and-half in a blender. Blend to a smooth purée. Pour purée into a pan or bowl. Heat chicken broth to boiling. Slowly add hot broth to purée. May be served hot or cold. If serving hot, heat, but do not let it boil. If serving cold, refrigerate for several hours and serve in cold bowls. Garnish with a dollop of sour cream.

~ BROWN POTATO SOUP

6 medium potatoes, peeled
    and diced
1 medium onion, chopped
Water
2½ cups skinned, chopped
    tomatoes
4 tablespoons flour (oat, rice,

or wheat, depending on
    sensitivities)
2 tablespoons butter (use oil
    if sensitive to milk)
Salt and freshly ground
    pepper
Basil

Place potatoes and onion in saucepan; add water to cover. Bring to a boil and simmer for 15 minutes. Add tomatoes and simmer 5 minutes more. Brown flour in butter, stir into simmering vegetable mixture. Season with salt, pepper, and basil. Serves 6.

∽ LEEK AND POTATO SOUP

6 leeks
6 potatoes

1 quart soup stock (beef or
   chicken)

Cook leeks and potatoes until tender. Blend and add to soup stock. Cook till heated through. Serves 6.

∽ THICK AND DELICIOUS YOGURT SOUP

¼ cup chopped onion
¼ cup butter (or margarine
   or oil)
3 tablespoons flour
1 teaspoon crushed herbs
   (thyme, chives, savory)
2 cups light cream or milk
   (goat's milk or soy milk
   may be used in place of
   cow's milk)

2 cups chicken or vegetable
   broth
8-ounce carton plain yogurt
2 egg yolks, beaten
1 cup asparagus, parboiled
1 cup mushrooms, sautéed
Green and red pepper slices
   (optional)

Sauté onion in butter until tender but not brown. Stir in flour and crushed herbs. Gradually stir in light cream or milk and broth. Cook and stir over medium heat till slightly thickened. Reduce heat and simmer, uncovered, for 5 minutes. Combine yogurt and egg yolks. Stir 1 cup of cream mixture into yogurt; return to pan. Cook and stir over medium heat until thickened, do not boil. Reduce heat and cook for 2 minutes. Stir in asparagus and mushrooms. Remove from heat. Blend mixture in blender or food processor until smooth. May heat through or serve chilled. (If too thick, add milk to desired consistency.) Garnish with green and red pepper slices, if desired. Makes 6 servings.

∽ MEXICAN COTTAGE CHEESE CAKES

3 cups small-curd creamed
  cottage cheese
4 large eggs
2 cups bread crumbs (wheat,
  potato, rice, or barley,
  depending on sensitivities)

2 tablespoons butter (or
  margarine or oil)
2 tablespoons corn oil

In a large bowl, mix cottage cheese, 2 of the eggs, and 1 cup of the crumbs. Beat the remaining 2 eggs in a shallow plate and put the remaining 1 cup of crumbs in another plate. Divide cottage cheese mixture into 8 portions, using a scant ½ cup for each. Shape into patties about ¾ inch thick (the mixture may be soft and difficult to handle). Dip each patty into the beaten eggs and then into crumbs to coat completely. Let stand 15 minutes. In a heavy skillet, heat 1 tablespoon each of butter and oil over moderate heat. When butter is melted, add patties and cook 3 minutes on each side. Cook remaining patties in remaining butter and oil. Serve with Mexican Sauce (following recipe).

∽ MEXICAN SAUCE

2 tablespoons butter (or
  margarine or oil)
½ cup chopped green pepper

1 cup sliced mushrooms
Two 8-ounce cans tomato
  sauce

In a small saucepan melt butter over moderately high heat. Add green pepper and cook 2 minutes, stirring frequently. Add mushrooms and cook 1 minute longer, stirring constantly. Add tomato sauce and heat to boiling.

⌒ ROAST POULTRY AND BEEF

Place the beef or chicken on a rack in an open pan. Do not add water and do not cover. Bake at 300°–350°F 20—30 minutes per pound. The meat thermometer should read for beef: rare 140°F, medium 150°F, well done 180°F.

Variation: Steaks, veal, and chicken may also be broiled on this day according to your favorite method.

⌒ BROCCOLI SOUFFLE

2 tablespoons chopped onion
3 tablespoons butter (or
　margarine or oil)
3 tablespoons flour
　(whatever variety is
　allowable for you)

⅓ cup milk (cow, goat, or
　soy)
1 cup grated Cheddar cheese
2 eggs, separated
1 large bunch broccoli

In a large skillet, sauté onion in butter. Add flour and stir to a pasty consistency. Add milk slowly and stir till smooth. Add cheese and stir till cheese melts. Add beaten egg yolks and cool. Carefully fold in beaten egg whites. Pour over broccoli and bake at 350°F for 30 minutes.

⌒ OVEN-BROWNED CHEESE

6–8 cups ricotta cheese,
Corn oil for greasing plate

3 teaspoons freshly ground
　black pepper

Preheat the oven to 400°F. Mound ricotta cheese into greased 9-inch stoneware pie plate. With fingers force black pepper randomly into sides and top of ricotta cheese about 1 inch deep. Sprinkle top and sides with additional pepper. Bake for 2–3 hours, or until cheese is dark brown. Darkness enhances flavor. Store in a cool place. Slice into wedges to serve.

∿ DUTCH CHEESE TART

8 ounces Edam cheese
1 cup bread crumbs (rice,
   wheat, corn, etc.,
   depending on sensitivities)
¼ cup plus 1 tablespoon

butter, (or margarine)
   melted
3 medium tomatoes
6–8 mushrooms

Shred 4 ounces of the cheese; cut remaining cheese into slices. Blend cheese, crumbs, and ¼ cup of the butter. Line a 9-inch pie plate with this mixture. Layer cheese slices, tomatoes, and mushrooms. Top with the remaining tablespoon of butter. Bake at 350°F for 20 minutes.

∿ LO-CAL CREAMY DRESSING

1 cup cottage cheese
⅓ cup buttermilk or yogurt

¼ teaspoon garlic powder
   (optional)
Chopped chives

Blend all ingredients except chives until smooth. Add chopped chives after blending. Serve on baked potatoes.

∿ ROASTED PEPPERS

1 large green pepper
1 large red pepper
1 garlic clove, crushed

Corn oil
Basil

Place whole peppers under preheated broiler until skins are black. Remove from oven and place in a brown bag. When peppers are cool, carefully remove skins and tops along with seeds. Rinse with cold water. Place in a flat dish and sprinkle generously with garlic, oil, and basil to taste. Marinate a few hours or overnight. Slice into strips.

∽ BAKED EGGPLANT

1 eggplant
2 eggs
¾ cup bread crumbs (rice,
* wheat, corn, etc.,*
* depending on sensitivities)*

1 onion, chopped
Freshly ground black pepper
Butter

Peel and cube eggplant; steam till tender. Mash and mix with eggs, ½ cup of the bread crumbs, onion, and pepper. Place in a casserole. Mix the remaining ¼ cup of bread crumbs with butter and sprinkle over eggplant. Bake at 350°F for 45 minutes.

∽ MUSHROOM BURGERS

2 cups chopped mushrooms
1 tablespoon butter (or
* margarine)*
Cayenne pepper to taste
1 egg, beaten

¼ cup chopped onion
¼ cup chopped green pepper
1 cup whole-wheat bread
* crumbs*
Butter or oil for frying

Sauté mushrooms in butter; season with pepper. Place mushrooms in bowl with beaten egg, add onion, pepper, and crumbs. Shape into patties. Add more bread crumbs if needed to hold together. Fry patties in butter. Serve in pocket bread with tomatoes and mayonnaise.

Variation: Put a slice of cheese on top of patties and place under broiler until cheese is melted.

∿ MUSHROOM CASSEROLE

1 onion, sliced
1 tablespoon butter
1 pound mushrooms,
 chopped
2 hard-boiled eggs, sliced
1 cup bread crumbs (wheat,

oat, rice, depending on
 sensitivities)
Basic Cream Sauce (see
 following recipe)
½ cup grated Cheddar
 cheese

Sauté onion in butter. In a buttered casserole dish, layer mushrooms, eggs, and bread crumbs. Add onion to cream sauce, and pour in casserole. Top with grated cheese. Bake at 300°F for 30 minutes.

∿ BASIC CREAM SAUCE

2 tablespoons butter (or
 margarine)
2 tablespoons flour (wheat,
 oat, potato, rice, depending
 on sensitivities)

1 cup milk (cow, goat, or soy)
Dash of pepper
½ teaspoon salt

In saucepan, melt butter at low temperature. Remove pan from heat; stir in flour. Blend to paste. Return to heat and slowly add milk. Stir till thick. Season to taste.

Variation: For cheese sauce, add 1 cup grated cheese after sauce thickens.

∿ ROASTED EGGPLANT

1 large eggplant, unpeeled
5 cloves garlic

Corn oil

Preheat the oven to 350°F. Cut 5 slits lengthwise in whole eggplant. Cut cloves of garlic in half. Place 2 halves of garlic in each "pocket" of eggplant. Lay eggplant in an oiled baking dish. Sprinkle top with oil. Bake for about 20 minutes. Cool. Remove skin of eggplant and place the remainder into serving dish. Serve with toasted slices of bread if allowed.

∽ TOMATO AND EGGPLANT CASSEROLE

4 tomatoes, sliced
1 medium eggplant, peeled
  and cubed

1 onion, chopped
1 tablespoon garlic extract or
  powder

Combine all ingredients in a casserole and bake at 350°F for 45–60 minutes. May also be steamed.

∽ SAUTEED EGGPLANT

½ cup corn (or other) oil
1 large eggplant, peeled and
  cubed
1 onion, chopped

1 clove garlic, crushed
3 small tomatoes, chopped
1 can (6 ounces) tomato paste

In a large saucepan, heat oil. Add eggplant, onion, and garlic. Cover pan and cook over medium heat for 10 minutes. Add tomatoes and tomato paste. Simmer for 20 minutes. Makes 6 servings.

∽ MUSHROOMS AND EGGPLANT

2 tablespoon butter (or
  margarine)
1 large onion, chopped
½ pound mushrooms, sliced

1 medium eggplant, peeled
  and cubed
½ cup water
½ clove garlic, crushed

In a saucepan, melt butter. Add onion. Cook until limp. Add mushrooms. Cook for 5 minutes. Add eggplant, water, garlic. Cover pan. Cook over low heat until vegetables are tender.

∽ BAKED FRENCH FRIES

6 potatoes   *6 tablespoons corn oil*

Pare and cut potatoes lengthwise in 8 to 12 strips. Soak in cold water while fixing. Place the strips of potato in a shallow pan; they should not touch each other. Pour corn oil over. Bake in the lower part of a very hot oven (450°F) for 20 minutes or until the strips are brown on the bottom. Turn and cook until brown and tender. Makes 6 servings.

∽ GOLDEN CHEESE

1 pint cherry tomatoes, halved
1 tablespoon butter (or margarine), melted
12 ounces Gruyère cheese
1 cup fine dry bread crumbs (wheat, oat, rice, etc., depending on sensitivities)

3 tablespoons flour (wheat, oat, rice, etc., depending on sensitivities)
2 eggs, well beaten
Corn oil for deep fat frying

In a skillet, sauté tomatoes in butter for 1 to 2 minutes; set aside. Cut cheese into ½-inch-thick squares about 4 × 4 inches; cut each square diagonally to form 2 triangles. Combine bread crumbs and flour. Dip cheese triangles into beaten egg, then into bread crumb mixture. Let stand a few minutes to dry. Dip cheese in egg, then in crumbs again; chill to set coating. Heat oil to 375°F. Fry cheese quickly until golden brown, about 1 to 2 minutes. Drain on paper toweling. Garnish cheese with sautéed tomatoes. Makes 4–6 servings.

∾ EGGPLANT PARMIGIANA

2 tablespoons corn oil
½ cup chopped onion
1 clove garlic, crushed
1-pound can tomatoes
6-ounce can tomato paste
2 teaspoons oregano

1 teaspoon basil
1 large eggplant
1¼ cups grated Parmesan
  cheese
8 ounces mozzarella cheese,
  sliced

In hot oil, sauté onion and garlic. Add tomatoes, tomato paste, oregano, basil, and 1 cup of water. Bring to boiling. Reduce heat; simmer, uncovered, for 20 minutes. Do not peel eggplant. Cut eggplant crosswise into slices ½ inch thick. Arrange half of the eggplant slices in bottom of 13 × 9-inch baking dish. Sprinkle with half of the Parmesan cheese. Top with half of the mozzarella cheese. Top with half of the tomato sauce. Arrange remaining eggplant slices over tomato sauce. Cover with rest of Parmesan cheese, tomato sauce, and mozzarella. Bake at 350°F for 45–60 minutes. Makes 6 servings.

∾ CHICKEN FRIED RICE

2 tablespoons corn oil
1 medium onion, diced fine
⅔ cup of chicken breast, cut
  into bite-size pieces

2 eggs, beaten
6 cups cold, cooked rice

Heat oil, fry onion till transparent; add chicken and stir once or twice. Add eggs and stir till they begin to set. Add rice and stir till heated through and separated nicely.

Breads and Desserts

᠆ MILLET CORN BREAD

1 cup cornmeal
1 cup millet flour
1 teaspoon baking powder
Dash of salt

1 egg, beaten
3 tablespoons corn oil
1 cup milk (cow, goat, or soy)

Mix all ingredients lightly. Pour into greased pie plate or muffin tin. Bake at 450°F for 25 minutes.

᠆ BARLEY BREAD

2 eggs
2½ cups milk (cow, goat, or soy)
3 tablespoons clover honey

2 tablespoons corn oil
2½ cups barley flour
2 teaspoons baking powder

Separate eggs. Beat whites to stiff peaks. In another bowl beat egg yolks, milk, honey, and oil. Then add flour and baking powder. Stir till completely mixed. Place beaten egg whites on top of barley mixture. With spoon fold in whites; do not stir or beat. Place in large loaf pan. Bake at 350°F for 1 hour.

᠆ GINGERBREAD

2½ cups whole wheat flour
1 teaspoon ginger
½ teaspoon cinnamon
1 cup molasses

½ cup corn oil
½ cup boiling water
¼ cup raisins

Preheat the oven to 350°F. In a medium bowl, mix well flour, ginger, and cinnamon. In another bowl mix well molasses, oil, and water. Add to flour mixture. Stir just until smooth. Stir in raisins. Turn into well-greased 9-inch square pan. Bake for 55–60 minutes. Cool in pan on rack. Cut in squares to serve.

∼ BROWN RICE MUFFINS

1 cup brown-rice flour
1½ teaspoons baking powder
1 egg, beaten
½ cup milk (cow, goat, or
   soy)

4 tablespoons corn oil
¼ cup clover honey
¼ cup raisins (optional)

Sift dry ingredients. Beat egg and blend lightly with milk, oil, and honey. Blend, do not beat. Add raisins, if desired. Bake at 450°F in well-greased muffin tins for 15 minutes. Makes 6 large or 12 small muffins.

∼ BRAN MUFFINS

1 cup whole wheat flour
1 cup bran
2 teaspoons baking powder
½ teaspoon salt

1 egg
3 tablespoons honey
3 tablespoons corn oil
1 cup milk (cow, goat, or soy)

Mix dry ingredients, beat egg, add honey, oil, and milk. Stir only enough to mix. Bake at 425°F in well-greased muffin tins for 15 minutes.

∼ DATE-NUT BARS

2 cups whole wheat flour
2 teaspoons baking powder
2 cups butter (or margarine)
2 eggs
2 tablespoons water

2 cups shredded,
   unsweetened coconut
2 cups chopped chestnuts or
   other nuts
2 cups pitted, chopped dates

Preheat the oven to 350°F. Stir together flour and baking powder. In another bowl, beat together butter, eggs, and 1 tablespoon of the water. Add flour mixture and mix well. Mix together coconut, nuts, dates, and the remaining tablespoon of water. Add to batter, mixing well. Press mixture into lightly greased 15½ × 10½ × 1-inch baking sheet, or two 8-inch square pans. Bake for 15–20 minutes or until done. Makes about 60 bars.

∽ OATMEAL CRACKERS

1 tablespoon clover honey　　*1 cup water*
½ cup corn oil　　　　　　　*4 cups oatmeal*

Blend honey, oil, and water. Stir in oatmeal. Mix well. Dough should be stiff. Chill. Roll out, cut into squares. Bake at 350°F for about 20 minutes. Makes 2 dozen crackers.

Ideas for Snacks

∽ POPCORN MUNCHIES—3 WAYS
PLAIN POPCORN #1

3 tablespoons corn oil　　*½ cup popping corn*

Pour oil into a large, heavy skillet with tight-fitting lid. Sprinkle the popping corn into the oil. Cover skillet. Heat slowly, shaking skillet gently as soon as corn begins to pop and continuing until popping stops. Pour popped corn into a large bowl. If allowed, top with melted butter.

∽ CURRIED #2

3 tablespoons corn oil　　　*1 teaspoon curry powder*
½ cup popping corn　　　　*1 cup raisins*
2 tablespoons butter (or
　margarine)

Prepare popping corn as in preceding recipe. After pouring into bowl, melt butter in a small saucepan until it bubbles but does not brown. Add curry powder and stir. Add raisins to popcorn in bowl, drizzle butter mixture over, and toss until well coated.

∽ SEASONED #3

1 tablespoon corn oil
3 cups popped corn
½ teaspoon chopped chives

1 teaspoon grated Parmesan
    cheese

Heat oil in heavy skillet. Add popped corn and seasonings and toss until well heated, about 5 to 7 minutes. Serve at once.

∽ COCONUT KISSES

3 egg whites
½ cup clover honey

2 tablespoons cornstarch or
    potato flour
3 cups shredded coconut

Beat egg whites till stiff. Add honey a little at a time. When stiff and glossy add flour a little at a time. Place mixture in a double boiler over hot (not boiling) water and simmer 15 minutes, beating constantly. Add coconut to egg mixture and keep in double boiler 15 minutes longer. Drop by teaspoonfuls onto a greased pan and bake in a moderate oven (325°F) until light brown and dry, about 10 to 15 minutes.

∽ CORN CHIPS

½ cup cornmeal
1⅓ cups water

2 tablespoons corn oil

Mix cornmeal with about ½ of the water to make paste. Pour remaining water into top of double boiler, set over direct heat, and bring to a boil. Blend in cornmeal paste, stir until smooth. Add oil and stir again. Cover. Place over hot water. Simmer 30 minutes. Turn mixture into two oiled 9 × 9-inch pans and spread out ¼ inch thick. Bake at 425°F for about 50 minutes until light brown and crisp. Cut into 1-inch squares.

Day No. 2	—Allowable Foods
Rose	Plum, prune, cherry, peach, apricot, nectarine, almond, apple, pear, quince
Mulberry	Mulberry, fig
Carrot	Parsnips, carrots, celery, celeriac, dill, celery seed
Parsley	Parsley
Sapucaia	Brazil nut
Cashew	Cashew, pistachio, mango
Arrowroot	Arrowroot
Bellflower, Thistle	Lettuce, chicory, endive, escarole, artichoke, sunflower seed and oil, safflower oil
Mammal	Pork
Mollusks	Abalone, snail, squid, clam, mussel, oyster, scallop
Bony Fish	Tuna, cod, haddock, hake
Farinosa	Pineapple
Honey	Tupelo honey

ROTARY DIET DAY NO. 2

Juices

∽ CARROT JUICE

Carrots are an excellent source of vitamin A. Select fresh carrots and if necessary cut to fit in a juicer. Always drink juices within seven minutes of making them.

∽ CELERY JUICE

Prepare as in preceding recipe.

∼ APPLE-ADE

6 apples   *Tupelo honey to taste*
Water to cover

Peel and quarter apples. Cover with water and simmer until tender. Mash to a pulp in the water. Sweeten to taste with honey. Add enough water to make 6 full glasses. This is very good with mineral water.

∼ CASHEW COOLER

8 tablespoons crushed   *4 tablespoons tupelo honey*
cashews   *4 cups fresh apple, apricot,*
4 cups water   *or pear juice*

Combine all ingredients in blender. Strain. Chill before serving. Makes 8 servings.

∼ CARROT HEALTH DRINK

2 medium carrots, sliced   *1 apple, peeled, cored and*
1½ cups pineapple (or peach *cut into eighths*
or pear) juice   *2 tablespoons tupelo honey*

Place all ingredients in blender and blend until smooth. Serve chilled with a carrot swizzle stick. Makes 3 cups.

Breakfast Ideas

∼ BLENDER APPLESAUCE

Apples   *Tupelo honey (optional)*
Water

Dice apples. Peel only if waxed. Add a few pieces at a time to blender container. Purée, adding enough water to get the machine going. Sir in small amount of tupelo honey, if desired. Use immediately to insure maximum vitamin retention and to prevent browning.

∽ FRESH PINEAPPLE

Select a pineapple that is golden brown in color, soft to the touch, and sweet smelling. With a large, sharp knife, cut the pineapple into 1-inch slices, starting at the bottom to enable you to use the top as a hand hold. Using a smaller sharp knife, peel each slice and remove any eyes that might remain. Cut in half and remove core. Use in half slices or cut into 1-inch cubes, as desired. If your pineapple is ripe and your knife is sharp, this whole process can be completed in 5 minutes.

∽ BROILED FRESH PINEAPPLE

1 whole fresh pineapple   *2 teaspoons butter (or*
2 teaspoons tupelo honey   *margarine)*

Slice pineapple, skin and all, into ½-inch slices. Peel the slices and cut out the eyes. Place on a buttered baking sheet, drizzle honey over the slices, and dot with butter. Broil about 5 to 7 minutes or until slightly browned. Makes 4 servings.

∽ STUFFED FIGS

Figs   *Almonds*
Tupelo Honey

Preheat oven to 350°F. Cut each fig three-fourths of the way around without disturbing stem. Open fig, moisten inside with honey. Insert nut and squeeze together to seal. Moisten fig with honey. Place on oiled cookie sheet. Bake until fork tender.

Salads and Main Dishes

✓ GRATED CARROT SALAD

2 cups grated carrots
1 cup chopped celery

1 teaspoon apple juice
1 teaspoon safflower oil

Mix all ingredients together.

✓ PINEAPPLE AND CELERY SALAD

1 cup diced celery
1 cup chopped pineapple
  meat

Sunflower seeds

Mix ingredients together and serve on lettuce leaves with Nut Dressing (following recipe).

✓ NUT DRESSING

4 tablespoons sunflower oil
2 tablespoons tupelo honey

Ground almonds

Mix ingredients together well.

✓ PICKLED CARROT SALAD

4 teaspoons safflower oil
¼ cup apple cider vinegar
2 teaspoons tupelo honey

1 pound carrots, shredded or
  grated

Mix first 3 ingredients in a salad bowl. Add grated carrots and toss.

~ SWEET AND CRUNCHY CARROTS

4 medium carrots
1 cup pineapple juice
1 teaspoon tupelo honey

2 tablespoons chopped
almonds

Wash carrots and remove tops. Cut into ¼-inch slices and place in a skillet. Add the pineapple juice and honey and simmer, covered, until barely tender. Sprinkle with almonds, which may be toasted until lightly browned, and serve.

~ TUNA-STUFFED ARTICHOKE BOTTOMS

2 cooked artichoke bottoms
(fresh or canned)

3½-ounce can of water-
packed tuna
Sunflower seeds

Fill artichoke bottoms with tuna. Sprinkle with sunflower seeds.

~ ROAST PORK

Place the roast on a rack in an open pan or stand it on the ribs with the fat side up. Season with allowable herbs and spices. Add no water. Do not cover and do not baste. Roast at 350°F for 20 minutes per pound. Cook until meat thermometer reads 170°F.

~ BROILED OR STEAMED SEAFOOD

The following fish may be steamed for Day 2: clams, mussels, abalone, oysters, and squid.
The following fish may be broiled for Day 2: scallops, cod, haddock, and hake.
Water-packed tuna may also be eaten on this day.

Desserts

∽ APRICOT SAUCE

*¾ cup diced, dried apricots
   (soaked overnight)
⅓ cup tupelo honey*

*1½ cups water or soaking
   juice from apricots*

Cook apricots, honey, and water in heavy saucepan, over low heat, for about 30 minutes. Cool slightly, then process in blender until smooth. If necessary, add water or more apricot juice to obtain right consistency. Cool completely, put into sealed container, and store in refrigerator. Makes about 2 cups of sauce.

∽ FIG AND NUT SPREAD

*4 small figs
¼ cup chopped raw cashew
   nuts*

1 small apple, cored

Finely chop or blend all ingredients. A delicious spread on crackers.

∽ ALMOND CARROT MILK

*2 ounces almonds
1 carrot*

*8 ounces water
Tupelo honey to taste*

Combine ingredients in blender. Blend well together. Serve well chilled.

Ideas For Snacks

Pitted prunes stuffed with almonds or Brazil nuts.
Dried mixed fruit: apricots, peaches, prunes, pineapple, etc.

∿ CELERY SNACK

Celery
Nut butter—cashew or
almond (may make own in
blender or purchase at
health food store)

Wash celery, cut into 2-inch slices. Fill cavities with nut butter.

Day No. 3

	—Allowable Foods
Rose	Strawberry, raspberry, blackberry, loganberry, youngberry, boysenberry, rose hips
Carica	Papaya
Gooseberry	Currant, gooseberry
Brassica	Cabbage, cauliflower, broccoli, Brussels sprouts, turnips, rutabaga, kale, collard, kohlrabi, celery cabbage, radish, watercress, Chinese cabbage, horseradish
Mustard	Mustard, mustard greens
Nightshade	Sesame seed, sesame oil
Proendalium	Macadamia nut
Walnut	Black walnut, English walnut, hickory nut, pecan
Pink	Beet, spinach, chard
Morning Glory	Sweet potato
Mammal	Lamb
Bony Fish	Flounder, halibut, sole, grouper, seabass, red snapper, sardine, plaice
Honey	Wildflower

ROTARY DIET DAY NO. 3

Juices

∿ RAS-LEM SWIZZLE

1 quart fresh raspberries, or *½ cup wildflower honey*
* two 10-ounce packages* *1 cup warm water*
* frozen raspberies*   *2 quarts carbonated water*

Wash and drain fresh raspberries; put them in a saucepan with 1 cup of water, bring to a boil, and simmer for a minute. (If using frozen berries, no cooking is necessary. Just thaw before using.) Purée berries in blender and press through sieve to remove seeds. Dissolve honey in warm water, add carbonated water, raspberries and ice to chill. Serve in individual glasses with ice. Makes 12 servings.

∿ CABBAGE JUICE

Select firm fresh cabbage, the greener the better. Wash and cut into chunks that can be fed into a juicer. Always select vegetables with the deepest colors and those that are crisp, fresh, firm, and juicy.

∿ SPINACH JUICE

Prepare as in preceding recipe.

Breakfast Ideas

∿ BREAKFAST FRUIT

½ papaya   *Strawberries*

Scoop out papaya seeds. Fill with strawberries. Top with sesame tahini. Makes 1 serving.

∽ SESAME SEED MILK

½ cup sesame seeds   1 teaspoon wildflower honey
1½ cups water

Put sesame seeds and water in blender. Blend at high speed for 4–5 seconds, adding honey in droplets. Strain through cheesecloth. Makes 1 serving.

Salads and Main Dishes

∽ BEET SALAD

Spinach, chopped   Grated beets
Swiss chard, chopped

Mix ingredients together and serve with Nut Dressing (following recipe).

∽ NUT DRESSING

4 tablespoons olive oil   Ground nuts (walnuts,
2 tablespoons wildflower   pecans, or hickory nuts)
   honey   2 tablespoons papaya juice

Combine all ingredients and blend well.

∽ CABBAGE SOUP

4 cups water   1½ teaspoons sesame tahini
½ cabbage, with hard stem
   removed

Bring water to a boil, add cabbage, reduce heat and simmer, partially covered, for 50–60 minutes. Stir in sesame tahini. Makes 4 servings.

∽ ROAST LAMB

Coat crown roast or leg of lamb with mustard. Place the roast on a rack in an open pan or stand it on the ribs with the fat side up. Do not add water, do not cover, and do not baste. Roast at 325°F for 30–40 minutes per pound or until thermometer reads 180°F.

∽ BROILED LAMB

Choose tender meat one to two inches thick. Preheat the broiler to 400°–425°F. Broil the meat on one side, season, turn and broil on the other side.

∽ BROILED FISH

The following fish may also be broiled for Day 3: Flounder, halibut, plaice, sole, grouper, seabass, red snapper.

∽ JAPANESE CABBAGE

½ head white cabbage
1 cup water
8 teaspoons wildflower
  honey

1 teaspoon dry mustard
2 teaspoons sesame seeds

Shred the cabbage and place in a heavy pot with water. Cover and cook over medium heat for 8–10 minutes. Drain well. Stir in honey, mustard, and sesame seeds. Serve hot.

∽ ZESTY BEETS

2 cups cooked beets, whole,
  sliced, or diced
1 tablespoon nut butter or
  olive oil

1 tablespoon horseradish
¼ teaspoon mustard

Heat beets; drain. Melt nut butter. Add horseradish and mustard. Pour butter mixture over beets and toss.

∽ CABBAGE DELIGHT

3 cups thickly shredded
    cabbage
1½ cups cubed turnips
1½ cups Chinese or celery
    cabbage

2 cups water
1 tablespoon tupelo honey
¼ cup sesame oil

Combine all ingredients, cook gently until just tender.

∽ STIR-FRY VEGETABLES

Slice diagonally assorted vegetables such as: cauliflower, broccoli, celery cabbage, and Chinese cabbage. Heat small amount of sesame oil in wok or frying pan. Stir-fry vegetables till they change color. Garnish with sesame seeds or walnuts.

∽ TENDER TURNIPS

4–6 turnips   *1 tablespoon sesame oil*

Cook turnips till tender. Add sesame oil and mash till smooth. Makes 4 servings.

∽ ROASTED TURNIPS

4–6 turnips   *Sesame oil*

Peel and slice turnips. Place in a baking dish with a small amount of sesame oil. Bake at 350°F for about 30 minutes or until tender and brown.

Desserts

∼ SWEET POTATO SWEET

For each serving you will need:

1 baked sweet potato

1 tablespoon wildflower honey
2 tablespoons walnuts.

Remove potato from skin and mix with other ingredients. This tastes good in a nut crust. Serve hot or cold.

Ideas for Snacks

Dried papaya
Olives

Radishes
Mixed nuts

Day No. 4	Allowable Foods
Rue	Orange, grapefruit, lemon, lime, tangerine
Heath	Blueberry
Banana	Banana
Gourd	Pumpkin, squash, cucumber, cantaloupe, muskmelon, honeydew, watermelon, casaba, zucchini, acorn squash, spaghetti squash
Mallow	Cottonseed oil
Berch	Filbert, hazelnut
Crustaceans	Crab, crayfish, lobster, prawn, shrimp
Legume	Navy bean, lima bean, kidney bean, string bean, soybean, lentil, black-eyed pea, peanut, pinto bean, green pea, carob, soy oil, peanut oil, alfalfa sprouts
Honey	Orange honey
Buckwheat	Buckwheat
Orchid	Vanilla
Spurgel	Curry, tapioca, cassava, yucca
Myristicaceae	Nutmeg, mace
Bony fish	Salmon species, trout, swordfish
Honeysuckle	Cranberry

ROTARY DIET DAY NO. 4

Juices

∽ CRANBERRY JUICE

Wash berries, feed into juicer in handfuls, and push down with plunger. May be sweetened with a little orange honey.

∽ GRAPEFRUIT JUICE

Use a citrus juicer and make fresh grapefruit juice.

∽ ORANGE JUICE

Proceed as in preceding recipe.

Breakfast Ideas

∽ BUCKWHEAT PANCAKES AND BLUEBERRIES

1 cup buckwheat flour   *1 cup soy milk*
2 tablespoons soy flour   *1 tablespoon lecithin*
2 teaspoons baking powder *Blueberries*

Mix all ingredients except blueberries together. Fry on hot griddle. Top with orange honey and blueberries or Blueberry Sauce (following recipe).

∽ BLUEBERRY SAUCE

Blueberries   *Orange honey*
Orange juice   *1 tablespoon tapioca*

Mix blueberries in a saucepan with a small amount of juice, honey, and tapioca. Simmer till thick.

∽ SOY FLAKE CEREAL

2 cups water   *1 cup soy flakes*

Bring water to a boil. Add soy flakes and reduce heat. Simmer, covered, for 1 hour. Stir in the skins that rise to the top.

Salads and Main Dishes

∽ TOFU

There are many ways of using tofu. It may be stir-fried, deep-fried, or used plain in salads or sandwiches. Here is a quick, easy, and delicious way to serve tofu.

1½–2 tablespoons soy oil   *2 teaspoons soy sauce*
10–12 ounces tofu, cut
*   crosswise into ⅜-inch-thick*
*   slices*

Heat a skillet and coat with the oil. Add tofu slices and fry for 1 minute. Turn over slices, sprinkle with 1 teaspoon of the soy sauce and fry for 15–30 seconds more, or until nicely browned. Serve immediately while crisp and hot. Sprinkle with extra soy sauce to taste.

∽ STEAMED SHELLFISH

The following shellfish may be steamed on Day 4: crab, shrimp, lobster, crayfish, and prawns.

∽ BROILED FISH

The following fish may be brolied on Day 4: salmon, trout, and swordfish.

∽ BAKED SQUASH

1 medium butternut squash *Grated orange peel*
2 tablespoons orange honey *Nutmes*
3 tablespoons orange juice

Peel squash and cut into slices. Lay in a baking dish. In saucepan heat honey; pour over squash. Top with grated orange peel, orange juice, and sprinkle with nutmeg. Bake at 350°F for 45 minutes.

∽ ZUCCHINI-STUFFED SUMMER SQUASH

2 small summer squash *2 tablespoons cooked*
2 zucchini *buckwheat (kasha)*
  Peanut or soy oil

Wash vegetables and split lengthwise. Scoop out the summer squash and chop the center pieces. Chop the zucchini. Mix zucchini, squash, and buckwheat. Rub summer squash shells with oil and fill with squash mixture. Bake at 300°F for 45 minutes.

∽ SQUASH AND BEAN BAKE

2 or 3 acorn squash   *2 tablespoons orange honey*
1½ cups cooked beans (any
variety you prefer)

Cut squash in half, remove seeds. Place cut side down in a shallow baking pan. Pour about ½ inch boiling water into the pan. Cover and bake at 400°F for 45 minutes. Stir beans and honey together. Turn squash cut side up. Spoon beans into cavities. Bake, uncovered, for 15 minutes or until squash is tender. Makes 4–6 servings.

∽ FRENCH-FRIED ZUCCHINI

4 medium zucchini   *Soy oil*
Salt   *Soy flour*

Peel and cut ends off zucchini, cut into French-fry-size strips. Place on paper towel and salt. Let zucchini drain for at least 1 hour. Preheat deep fryer to 360°F. Rinse zucchini with water, dust with flour and submerge into deep fryer for 3–4 minutes or until golden brown. Drain on paper towels and serve immediately. Makes 4 servings.

∽ TOFU FRENCH FRIES

12 ounces firm tofu,   *Soy oil for deep-frying*

Slice tofu into strips. Heat oil to 350°F. Fry tofu slices till brown. Makes 2 servings.

∽ VEGETARIAN CHOPPED LIVER

Soy oil for cooking
1½ cups lentils, cooked

½ cup hazelnuts or pine
nuts
Soy sauce to taste

Coat skillet with oil. Add lentils and nuts. Mash and stir over heat until mixture thickens to a paste. Add soy sauce.

11

Cytotoxic Cookery

Cooking and meal preparing while on the Cytotoxic diet requires one constant rule: keep it simple. The fewer foods you use to prepare each meal, the easier it will be for you to stick to your rotary diet.

The Cytotoxic regimen will undoubtedly have you exploring new kinds of foods that will add variety and interest, as well as needed vitamins and minerals, to your diet. After a while you'll probably become quite inventive. The absence of food addictions and their inherent cravings mean that you will enjoy a greater variety of foods than ever before. Your mind won't always be leading you in the direction of one or two favorites, as it may have in the past.

To help you along, here are some cooking and meal-preparing hints provided by Ruth Kaufmann, who has been maintaining a rotating diet for her family of three. A debt of gratitude also goes to Sandy Gooch, owner of the most progressive health food store in the Los Angeles area, Mrs. Gooch's. Her store is at the leading edge of food sensitivity awareness, providing many food substitutes and loving advice for the growing number of people wishing to eliminate their incompatible foods.

BREAKFAST

- Make your own granola. Use 3 cups of either rolled oats, rye flakes, cornmeal, buckwheat groats, or wheat flakes. In a 9 × 39-inch pan, mix the grain with ½ cup oil and ½ cup either honey, maple syrup, or molasses. Add any of the following: 1 cup sunflower seeds, 1 cup sesame seeds, 2 cups chopped nuts, and ½ cup any kind of flour. Toast in 300° F oven for about 30 minutes. Mix with 1 cup raisins, chopped dates, or any dried fruit.
- Granola or dry cereal tastes great with fruit juice instead of milk.
- Millet is a good and much-overlooked grain. Try it as a breakfast cereal with honey and raisins.
- Millet or brown rice topped with poached eggs and fresh or dried herbs.
- For a change of pace, bake a potato for breakfast. Top it with fresh steamed spinach and a poached egg. Or top it with avocado and egg. Or melt cheese over it.
- For a light breakfast or good anytime snack, toast rice cakes (available at health food stores) and top with peanut butter, honey, or any nut butter and jam, or slice a banana over the nut butter and top with honey.
- Bake a yam or sweet potato for breakfast. Top with butter, toasted sesame seeds, and a little honey.
- Buckwheat is not wheat—it's in the same food family as rhubarb. To make buckwheat pancakes, mix 1 cup buckwheat flour, 1 egg, and 1 cup (soy, goat, or cow's) milk, then mix with 1 tablespoon honey and some fresh fruit. Add 1 teaspoon baking soda and cook on griddle. Top with honey, maple syrup, or fresh fruits.

- Stewed fruits are also good in the morning. Take any dried fruit (the unsulphured kind are best), cover with water, add thinly sliced lemon, lime, or orange, and bring to a boil. Simmer 1 hour or until fruits are puffed up and soft.
- Make a breakfast smoothie by whipping in a blender any fresh fruit, peeled—or frozen fresh fruit—with 1 cup papaya or any juice, 1 banana or frozen banana or fruit, and an ice cube. Blend until smooth.

OTHER MEALS

- Sprinkle toasted sesame or sunflower seeds on steamed vegetables. Grated fruit rinds—lemon, lime, or orange—also add an interesting flavor. A drop of sesame oil (available in the Chinese food section of the grocery store) adds a delightful taste and is a good replacement for butter.
- Tofu is a wonderful food made from soybeans. You can make tofu burgers by mixing together ½ cup tofu, 1 cup cooked beans, a dash of soy sauce (be careful if you're eliminating wheat, as most soy sauces contain wheat products), sesame or sunflower seeds, celery, onion, mushrooms. Form into patties and brown on both sides in the oil of your choice.
- Try sandwich spreads made from crushed split peas or chickpeas (garbanzo beans). Can be spread on bread or rice cakes and topped with sprouts, seeds, mayonnaise, celery, or onion.
- If you like pasta salads but are eliminating wheat, use spaghetti squash (available in most grocery stores).
- For a delicious snack, mix peanut or any nut butter, honey, puffed rice or millet, seeds, raisins; roll into balls and refrigerate.
- To make wheatless "bread crumbs," blend rice cakes or potato chips in a blender.
- Instead of pastry shells for creamed mixtures, try putting them in tomato, squash, or green pepper "shells."

- To make a piecrust from nuts, mix 1½ cups ground nuts with 3 tablespoons honey and press into a greased 9-inch pie pan. Fill with any fruit filling.
- Nut milk is a delicious milk replacer that children love. Place 1 cup nuts, 2 cups water, and 2 teaspoons honey in a blender. Blend until smooth. Cashews and almonds make very good nut milk.
- To sprout seeds—alfalfa, wheat berries, mustard, cabbage, sesame, lentils, soybeans, mung beans, or sunflower seeds—dampen sponge dishclothes and place on a cookie sheet. Arrange the beans or seeds in the wafflelike depressions. Cover the pan loosely with waxed paper and place in an unlit oven. Sprinkle a small amount of water on the seeds every day and leave covered until sprouted (a few days). Sprouting jars can also be purchased in most grocery stores, along with seeds for sprouting.
- Make tapioca pudding with fruit juice instead of milk. Quick tapioca box has recipe.
- Use pure broth in sauces and gravies instead of milk.
- One tablespoon artificially flavored Jello mix equals 1 tablespoon plain gelatin or agar-agar and 2 cups fruit juice and fresh fruit.

Food Substitutions

Food substituting is the backbone of a successful ongoing rotary diet. With a bit of experimenting, many ordinary recipes can be adapted to Cytotoxic cookery. While many people wisely choose to go on a "caveman diet" for the first two months of eliminating toxic foods—eating only raw fruits, vegetables, nuts and plain cooked meats, poultry, and fish—others find it difficult to switch to such an "uninteresting" diet for any length of time. If you are part of the latter group, use the following substitution lists to alter your favorite recipes. Remember, though, when on a rotation diet, it's important to keep recipes down to only a few ingredients, so you can keep track of your foods from day to day.

WHEAT SUBSTITUTES

1 cup wheat flour equals:

1⅓ cups rolled oats
⅔ cup oat flour
1 cup rye meal
1¼ cups rye flour
¾ cup soy flour   or
⅝ cup potato-starch flour
⅞ cup rice flour
½ cup barley flour
¾ cup cornmeal

½ cup rye flour plus
   ½ cup potato flour
⅝ cup rice flour plus
   ⅓ cup potato flour

Note: Cook these flours at lower temperatures and for a longer period of time than you would use for wheat flour. The end products usually tend to be crustier and crumblier than wheat products.

For thickening sauces and gravies, *1 tablespoon wheat flour equals:*

½ tablespoon cornstarch
½ tablespoon potato-starch flour
½ tablespoon rice flour
½ tablespoon arrowroot
2 teaspoons quick tapioca

Hint: For breading chops or extending meat loaf, try grinding rice cakes or use toasted oats or cornmeal. To toast oats, place 1 or 2 cups rolled oats on a cookie sheet and bake at 350°F until golden brown (15–20 minutes). Store in refrigerator.

YEAST SUBSTITUTES

It's impossible to avoid completely all yeast products, as yeast spores are in the very air we breathe and they grow rapidly in any food containing carbohydrates and water. Yeast comes in the general forms of bakers', brewers', compressed, dry, and natural. Yeast is used in breads as a leavening to release carbon dioxide and make it rise.

Vinegars contain yeast used for fermentation, as do all wines, beers, and any fermented product. Yeast is also used in many vitamins as a source of B vitamins. You can substitute baking soda and powder—1 teaspoon each for bakers' yeast to make bread rise. The end product will vary in taste or texture, but it will rise.

MILK SUBSTITUTES

Milk products are everywhere. Read labels for the following disguised milk products: lactose, caseinate or sodium caseinate or casein, lactalbumin, lactoglobulin, curds, whey.

Note that a milk sensitivity doesn't always mean that all dairy products have to be discarded. The Cytotoxic test lists separate reactions for butter, various cheeses, cow's milk, goat milk, and yogurt. I am reactive to cow's milk, yogurt, and Parmesan cheese, but can eat other dairy products. When self-testing, be sure to try each dairy product individually. Replace cow's milk with goat milk, evaporated goat milk, soy milk, or nut milk.

For infants, human breast milk is, of course, the best food to offer. There are breast milk banks that sell human milk to mothers unable to nurse their babies. There are also baby formulas available without cow's milk, but mothers should be cautioned to shop carefully, ideally seeking the advice of a nutritionist.

SUGAR SUBSTITUTES

1 cup cane sugar equals:
¾ cup honey (Reduce liquid in recipe by ¼ cup for every cup of sugar called for and bake at 25°F lower oven temperature than instructions call for.)

¾ cup pure maple syrup (Reduce liquid in recipe by 2 tablespoons.) (Be careful of grocery store "pancake syrups." They are not pure maple syrups, but rather a sugary conglomeration of corn syrup and artificial colors, additives, etc. Read labels!)

1 cup date sugar (To keep date sugar soft, store in a covered container with a piece of bread.)

CHOCOLATE SUBSTITUTES

1 cup cocoa (chocolate powder) equals:
1 cup carob powder
1 square baking chocolate equals:
3 tablespoons carob powder plus 1 tablespoon vegetable oil (Carob is high in natural sugar, so use less sweetener than recipe calls for.)

EGG SUBSTITUTES

There are no good substitutes for eggs on dishes like sponge cakes that require stiffly beaten egg whites, but many other recipes can be altered to eliminate eggs.

Baking powder contains eggs, so substitute 1½ teaspoons cream of tartar and ½ teaspoon baking soda for 1 teaspoon baking powder.

For custard, substitute 1 tablespoon cornstarch or potato starch for each egg. For general recipes, substitute 1 tablespoon vegetable oil and 2 tablespoons water for each egg.

CORN SUBSTITUTES

Corn is one of the most difficult foods to eliminate from the diet because it finds its way, often disguised, into many thousands of food preparations. Avoiding corn means going on a "caveman diet" or being an avid label reader. A curious note about corn sensitivity is that many people are able to eat fresh corn on the cob but cannot tolerate other corn products. It is thought that fresh corn is too rough to be fully digested, and thus the sensitivity isn't triggered.

When avoiding corn products, look for labels that say: corn flour, cornmeal, corn oil, cornstarch. The corn sugars are: Cerilose, dextrose, Dyno. Corn syrups are: Cartose, glucose, Karo, Puretose, Sweetose. Other corn products are grits, hominy, parched corn, and popped corn.

In addition, postage stamps, and envelope seals contain corn products.

Subsutitute molasses, sorghum, or honey for corn syrup. Substitute potato starch, arrowroot, or tapioca for cornstarch. Safflower oil most closely approximates corn oil for cooking purposes, but you can also use coconut, olive, peanut, or sunflower oils, or butter.

VITAMIN AND MINERAL SUPPLEMENTATION

The Cytotoxic diet, or any diet for that matter that eliminates many foods, can be deficient in some vitamins and minerals. Many people find it helpful to supplement their diets with vitamin and mineral supplements. I like to advise clients to get professional counseling for nutrient supplementation, as there are tests that can be administered to turn up any existing deficiencies.

We do know that vitamin C has been shown to be of value in the detoxification process during the initial five days of food withdrawal on the Food Sensitivity Diet (remember—*not* during any fasting period). People have noted a decrease in withdrawal symptoms, especially in the urge to smoke, with vitamin C supplementation. William Philpott, M.D., and Dwight Kalita, Ph.D., in their book, *Brain Allergies,* say that 20 to 30 grams of vitamin C per 24 hours can be tolerated without undue symptoms. Other vitamins, like B_6, pantothenic acid, calcium, vitamin A, and zinc are said to help the adrenal glands overcome the severe stress placed on them by food sensitivities and allergies.

Many doctors and nutritionists also prescribe amino acids to help assure the proper digestion of foods that are eaten. The charts below list the daily dietary allowances recommended for a 154-pound man by the Food and Nutrition Board of the National Research Council. These are the bare essentials needed for survival. The chart on page 178, on the other hand, lists the vitamin-mineral supplementation suggested by Roger J. Williams, Ph.D., in his book, *Physicians' Handbook of Nutri-*

tional Science. Whenever possible, a medical doctor or nutritionist should be consulted.

Table I

Daily dietary allowances recommended for a 154-pound man by the Food and Nutrition Board of the National Research Council.

Vitamin A	5,000 international units
Vitamin D	400 international units
Ascorbic Acid (Vitamin C)	45 milligrams
Thiamine	1.5 milligrams
Riboflavin	1.6 milligrams
Nicotinic Acid	18 milligrams (equivalent to the same amount of nicotinamide)
Folic Acid	0.4 milligrams
Pyridoxine	2.0 milligrams
Cyanocobalamin (Vitamin B$_{12}$)	0.003 milligrams
Vitamin E	15 international units

Table II

Vitamin and mineral supplements as suggested by Roger Williams, Ph.D.

Vitamin A	7,500 units	Calcium	250 milligrams
Vitamin D	400 units	Phosphate	750 milligrams
Vitamin E	40 units	Magnesium	200 milligrams
Vitamin M (menadione)	2 milligrams	Iron	15 milligrams
Vitamin C	250 milligrams	Zinc	15 milligrams
Thiamin	2 milligrams	Copper	2 milligrams
Riboflavin	2 milligrams	Iodine	0.15 milligrams
Vitamin B$_6$	3 milligrams	Manganese	5 milligrams
Vitamin B$_{12}$	0.009 milligrams	Molybdenum	0.1 milligrams
Niacinamide	20 milligrams	Chromium	1 milligram
Pantothenic acid	15 milligrams	Selenium	0.02 milligrams
Biotin	0.3 milligrams	Cobalt	0.1 milligram
Folic acid*	0.4 milligrams		
Choline	250 milligrams		
Inositol	250 milligrams		
Para-amino benzoic acid	30 milligrams		
Rutin	200 milligrams		

*Dr. Williams would recommend more folic acid (about 2 milligrams), but this conflicts with FDA regulations. Higher dosages are available under a doctor's prescription.

OTHER RECIPE SOURCES

There are some excellent food sensitivity/allergy cookbooks available at most bookstores that can be used in conjunction with your Food Sensitivity Diet. Remember that the success of the Food Sensitivity Diet depends on your ability to eliminate intolerant foods and rotate the rest. The best way to achieve this is to keep your meal preparation as simple and natural as possible. The fewer foods contained in any one recipe the easier it will be to rotate your foods properly. Many of the allergy cookbooks try to imitate "normal" recipes and therefore contain too many ingredients. It's possible to cut back on many of these recipes. When making bread, for instance, stay away from any recipe calling for three kinds of flour.

The recipe books listed below are all readily available at major bookstores.

Our favorite is *Coping with Food Allergy* by Dr. Claude A. Frazier. It contains valuable information on food substitutions. Only one complaint: the author suggests the use of processed meats, cheeses, and other questionable foods in some of the recipes and menu plans. On the positive side, each recipe is noted as "eggfree, milkfree," or "glutenfree, wheatfree," etc. This is most helpful for Cytotoxic dieters.

Dr. Mandell's Allergy-Free Cookbook by Fran Gare Mandell, M.S., is a follow-up to her husband's popular *Five Day Allergy Relief System*. Although I find that these recipes contain too many ingredients in most cases, they are well thought out. A nice feature of this book is that each recipe has a full list of substitute foods that can be used instead of those called for.

The *Allergy Cookbook and Food-Buying Guide* by Pamela P. Nonken and S. Roger Hirsch, M.D., is the most detailed work I've seen on the types of foods available for various eliminations. There are chapters on cooking without yeast, wheat, soy, milk, eggs, corn in which the author lists hundreds of foods that are suitable to eat by brand names or descriptions. The 300 recipes are kept short and simple, and the eliminated foods are listed next to each recipe. Many of the breads contain too many different kinds of flours to be useful on a rotary diet.

Allergy Cooking by Marion L. Conrad contains some worthwhile menus and cooking suggestions.

We found a surprising number of good elimination recipes in the popular *Joy of Cooking* by Irma S. Rombauer and Marion Rombauer Becker. For instance, there's a nice rice or potato flour sponge cake and a rice or potato flour brownie recipe. We didn't review all the popular "normal food" cookbooks, but we'd certainly suggest your scanning your home library for useful recipes.

The last word in keeping kids happy while avoiding sensitive foods is Dr. Lendon Smith's *Foods for Healthy Kids*. The book is crammed with useful information on childhood nutrition. The recipes are simple and basic, and a big plus is that each recipe notes the nutrients it contains. Some recipes are too long for rotary diets, but they can be easily simplified. I especially enjoyed the recipes for nutritious snacks, many of which contain only two or three ingredients.

There are some recipes and food-preparation hints in *Allergies and the Hyperactive Child* by Doris J. Rapp, M.D. The book also contains vitamin and mineral information.

12

The Food Sensitivity Weight-Loss Program

Despite the hundreds of best-selling weight-loss diets available today, more than half of all Americans are still overweight.

It's not that we don't want to be thin; that we don't desire the health, good looks, and energy that come with achieving our appropriate weight. Of course we want these things. In fact, weight loss has become somewhat of a national preoccupation, manifested in banner headlines that scream out at us from most major magazine covers. These headlines suggest all kinds of ways to fight our overweight conditions. Some of them are quite bizarre, others are amusing, and still others have proven harmful, even fatal, when followed over a long period of time.

When our diets fail us, we accuse ourselves of being a spoiled, pampered, overfed, and weak-minded society, unwilling to make even the smallest sacrifice on our own behalf. But

I don't think this is the case at all. The reason our diets don't work is that, until now, our doctors and weight loss specialists have been unable to accurately address the causes of weight gain. Without an understanding of the reasons for gaining weight, how can they presume to tell us how to lose it?

The causes of overweight in many people have become clear to us now, through Cytotoxic testing and food sensitivity/allergy research. We now know that in most people optimal weight maintenance can be achieved easily by eliminating the foods to which they are sensitive.

Next to the discovery of the Cytotoxic effect itself, the strongest clue to the mystery of chronic overweight is the recognition of our nutritional individuality. We each have a unique set of foods that are toxic to our bodies. It is this uniqueness that accounts for the fact that the weight-loss program that works for one person may not work for another— and never can work for everyone!

ADDICTION, NOT LAZINESS

Our overweight conditions are held in place by chemical addictions to our food sensitivities. Many of the foods we become addicted to are foods we eat every day, foods we have been taught to believe are good for us. Caught between the proverbial rock and hard place, overweight people feel their fat is the result of their own weak-mindedness and inability to control their eating. But we now know that overweight (and very often underweight as well) can be caused by the body's battle against its foreign invaders—more often than not the foods we enjoy the most.

If you are overweight, you have probably experienced the pain and frustration of trying to cut down on some of the foods you love to eat. I believe that overweight people tend to be too hard on themselves, feeling that they have a character flaw or weakness. The self-destructiveness and poor self-image that we often assume are the causes of overweight are actually only symptoms of a disease process. The disease is the food sensitivity's withdrawal-addiction syndrome, a phenomenon we have discussed at length in previous chapters.

If you are a compulsive eater, take a close look at your food needs. Does eating a small amount of your favorite food only make you feel hungrier? Do you sometimes even feel a bit shaky as you anticipate another delicious bite? Do you feel that no meal is complete without certain foods? If you try to do without one of your favorites, do you feel depressed? Tired? Confused?

These are withdrawal symptoms, and like any chemical dependency, the only thing that makes you feel better is to eat the craved-for food. Feeding the addiction keeps the withdrawal symptoms quiet.

The reason we don't ordinarily think in terms of food addiction in relation to overweight is that these withdrawal symptoms tend to be more subtle than the typical withdrawals related to alcohol or drug dependency. Sometimes a headache will occur, but usually one just experiences feelings of confusion, frustration, anger, depression, nervousness. Feelings, yes, but they are withdrawals all the same, and the sooner we recognize them as such, the sooner we will be able to cope with the problem.

Remember that addiction is an inherent quality of the food sensitivity process. Overweight is one of the body's responses to the toxic assault.

NEVER JUST FAT

It's extremely rare for symptoms to occur one at a time. Most of us have several working at the same time. Sensitivity-caused mental depression, for instance, might be accompanied by skin rashes and headaches; the person with painful joints might also complain of stomach problems.

An example of food sensitivity causing overweight along with other symptoms is the case of Jeannie, whose most debilitating problem was the migraine headaches that took over her life for three days and three nights twice each month. Not surprisingly, she was also more than fifty pounds overweight.

Jeannie began having a weight problem when she was about nine years old, and she entered high school weighing 178 pounds. During high school, though, she managed to drop her excess weight and got down to 118. Then, years later, after the birth of her first two daughters, she began to gain her weight back and to experience severe headaches. Since she had also started taking birth control pills, Jeannie thought her headaches might have been caused by the hormones in the pills. She also noticed that she'd get headaches around the time of her menstrual period each month, another possible explanation, according to her doctor.

Jeannie was introduced to the Cytotoxic test by a doctor she worked for. He thought her headaches, which were beginning to make her quite ill might be food-related. By this time, the twice-monthly migraines were leaving her an exhausted mess, depleted, and nervously anticipating the next siege of pain. She took the test, which showed a strong reaction to her favorite food, wheat, along with thirty-two other substances, among them all citrus fruits, barley, oats, and some vegetables.

During the first week of the elimination diet, her normal three-day migraine returned, but this time it was harsher than ever and lasted four days and nights. Fortunately, the doctor had warned her about possible withdrawal symptoms, and she persevered.

After the first week, her headaches disappeared, never to return. But the unexpected thing that happened to Jeannie was that her weight began to fall. She lost ten pounds the first week, and after four months on the diet had lost thirty-five pounds. Over an eight-month period, she lost fifty-two pounds and reports that she has no trouble keeping the weight off as long as she sticks to her diet. She is now able to maintain and enjoy an exercise program of long-distance cycling and square dancing that also contributes to her good health and stabilized weight.

I often hear stories like this from people who take the Cytotoxic test to get rid of symptoms other than overweight. People with sinus problems or painful joints are surprised to find they are also dropping weight. In Jeannie's case, she feels that the reason she was able to lose weight successfully, after failing with every fad diet she could find, is that she was so ill with her headaches that she stuck religiously to the Food Sensitivity Diet. "I had a lot of incentive," she told me. "If I wasn't so sick with those migraines and was only trying to lose weight, I don't know if I would have stayed with it."

I stress this need for total elimination of toxic foods in order to achieve weight loss, because experience has shown that overweight people tend to expect too much too soon, and often become quickly disenchanted with a particular weight-loss program.

Milton Gotlib, M.D., a weight-loss specialist, says that the psychological aspects of weight loss can be tricky.

> The psyche is a peculiar thing. People find out that their favorite foods are toxic to their systems and they know they should stop eating them. But we are very social creatures and are not always willing to give up our foods, and therefore part of our life-styles.
>
> I do notice, though, that even a partial elimination, while it may not cause much weight loss, will usually make the person feel better, more energtic, and sometimes that good feeling will motivate them to go a little further into the diet.

FOOD SENSITIVITIES AND FAT— THE CELLULAR REACTION

How do food sensitivities cause weight gain? The key to keeping weight down is keeping the foods we eat metabolizing well, feeding our cells, and not destroying them. Healthy cells don't retain water, causing weight gain. But cells that are assaulted by constant toxic attacks have all kinds of ways of trying to survive—and many of these ways cause us to gain weight or keep us from losing excess pounds.

In an optimum situation, our cells pick and choose from among the many food molecules floating past them. They take in those nutrients they need and then release their waste products. Unfortunately, this smooth transfer rarely gets to take place for any length of time. Instead, when sensitive foods are eaten, the substances floating by the cells are identified by them as toxic, and the cell begins performing all kinds of tricks to keep from getting poisoned, tricks that can and do cause weight gain. For many of us, obesity is the result of this cellular assault. Remember, the toxins can be apple, steak, string beans—anything the individual cell identifies as foreign.

One of the processes used by the cells to survive the toxic assault is water retention. As we discussed in Chapter 3, a cell will try to detoxify itself by taking on water when a toxic substance has passed through its membrane. By diluting what it considers poisonous, the cell has at least a chance to survive. In many cases, this water retention is the cause of a bloated, overweight feeling. It's the "water weight" that is usually the first large and gratifying chunk of weight to come off during the initial phase of a weight-loss diet. Unfortunately, in many diets, this is the only weight to come off, and the dieter is soon frustrated and unable to keep losing.

Cells also use water in another aspect of their battle against toxic substances—the ionization process. They must control what enters through their membranes and what gets out by way of waste products. Nutrients in, waste products out. The cell, therefore, has a permeable lining to allow this transfer to take place.

All food molecules are broken down into ions (negatively or positively charged atoms) during metabolism. The important thing to know about ions is that those with the same charge will repel each other, and those with opposing charges will attract each other. Thus, when a cell desires to keep certain ions from entering through its membrane, it takes on and ionizes water molecules, turning each molecule of water into a negative and positive ion. The cell will use a positive water atom to repel an unwanted positive ion outside the cell. It can be any kind of ion, say one of the chemical components of spinach or doughnut, but as long as it carries a positive charge, it will be repelled. Similarly, if the cell wishes to attract a desireable ion with a positive charge, it will use its negative water ion to pull it in, across the membrane.

This process takes a great deal of energy, and obviously, when there are many unwanted ions generated from the constant ingestion of sensitive foods, the cell must mass large quantities of water to keep this ionization battle going. Again, water retention occurs.

Poor metabolism, or incomplete digestion, is another result of the toxic assault. Foreign foods entering the body set up a stress situation that causes the pituitary gland to produce the hormone, ACTH (adrenocorticotropic hormone), which it uses to signal the adrenal glands to secrete steroids. Steroids are chemical messengers sent to various organs—in this case, mainly to the liver, instructing the organ to change its method of metabolism.

The liver responds to the steroids' stress command by decreasing its normal function of glucose catabolism (carbohydrate breakdown into sugars, which are turned into energy and then into the waste product, carbon dioxide, which is then breathed out through the lungs) to lipogenesis (turning carbohydrates into fatty acids, or lipids).

These fatty acids combine and form lipid globules, which are not water soluble. They can, therefore, float in the blood stream or become deposited in any organ or muscle. The liver is a vast storage organ for these lipids, which the body saves for possible future needs for extra body warmth or energy. But when there are too many fat globules produced, they can start causing problems. These stored or floating lipids are responsible for fat buildup, especially when stored under the skin layer.

The lipid globules can also get stuck in the arteries, clumping together and clogging the blood vessels, restricting the blood flow and causing atherosclerosis. It makes sense, therefore, that chubbiness and heart failure often accompany each other.

It's logical, also, to take a look at food sensitivities when trying to cure heart disease.

The fatigue that many overweight people feel is due in large part to the vast amounts of energy required by the cells to keep these various systems going while enduring constant toxic attack. Also, while all this is going on, the immune system's white blood cells are continuously being bombarded in the Cytotoxic effect, and more energy is expended.

What is happening is that the body is using a considerable amount of its energy resources simply to survive these food sensitivity assaults, and as a result, everything else suffers. The allergic threshold is lowered, allowing infections to enter and other symptoms to evolve.

Even the foods that are not sensitive to the system can't be properly digested, and the overweight condition is soon accompanied by an increasing number of other symptoms, like headaches, skin conditions, depression, etc.

Looking through the microscope at the Cytotoxic effect, it's easy to see that an overweight condition is a physiological problem that is far more encompassing than just eating too much food or not burning off enough calories. In fact, an ardent dieter can cut his calories down to the barest minimum needed for survival, and while he may drop some weight, we often find him gaining it right back as soon as he again eats foods to which he is sensitive.

Other dieters, and I have seen this happen many times, may eliminate all the high calorie foods they ever eat and still be unable to lose a single ounce of weight. Why? Because they are still consuming foods that are sensitive to their systems. These foods don't have to be high in calories to cause weight gain. They have only to trigger the mechanisms we've been discussing.

RE-OPTIMIZING—
LOSING WEIGHT AND KEEPING IT OFF

Reaching your body's optimum weight can be accomplished by taking three important steps. The success of each one depends on the fulfillment of the others.

First, *detoxify* your cells by isolating and eliminating your individual food sensitivities.

Then, *slim down* by getting rid of stored fats through exercise and by taking in specific nutrients that actually help the cells cleanse themselves.

Last, *cut the addiction syndrome* and keep new sensitivities from developing by rotating the foods remaining in your diet.

Detoxify.

To achieve weight loss that is not destructive to your body, weight loss that is permanent, that won't sap your energy, it's necessary to isolate and eliminate the foods to which your body is sensitive (see Chapter 9). After the initial water weight is dropped during the first week or so, you'll notice your weight coming off more slowly. Most doctors agree that this gradual loss of excess weight is more desirable than crash diets, as it gives the body a chance to adjust, not causing shock or confusion to the cells and organs.

Exercise and lose fat, not protein. As the weight comes off, most people notice increased energy, a desire for physical activity. I believe that any weight-loss program is made a hundred times easier when it's accompanied by some type of cardiovascular exercise. Dr. Gotlib encourages his dieting patients to begin some form of exercise—even twenty to thirty minutes a day is plenty—a brisk walk, a bike ride, anything that gets that heart pumping a bit faster. He cautions care and common sense, though. Straining the body is not the purpose of an exercise program.

The benefits of exercise in relation to weight loss are many. According to Gotlib, exercise releases free fatty acids, which are natural appetite suppressants. After a half-hour of aerobic exercise, there may be a feeling of thirst, but rarely is there hunger. People eat after exercise, he says, mostly because psychologically they want to reward themselves for the nice work they just did, not because they have an enormous appetite.

Another benefit of exercise is the release of various hormones that provide feelings of well-being or can promote restful sleep. "Ten minutes of exercise," writes Dr. Richard Passwater in his book, *Super-Nutrition for Healthy Hearts,* quoting the associate medical director for the Nationwide Insurance Company, "will double the blood level of norepinephrine, a hormone related to adrenalin, which boosts your spirits and destroys depression."

"Systematic exercising," Passwater says, ". . . eases stress, chases depression, improves sex, sleep and immunity, lowers blood cholesterol, strengthens bones, helps you think better and leaves you with a general feeling of well-being and alertness for 10 to 12 hours afterward." Anyone involved in a regular cardiovascular exercise program knows that these are not exaggerated claims.

Besides all these benefits, exercising also burns up calories, helping, in itself, to take off pounds.

The purpose of a weight-loss program is to help the body keep from retaining water and to get rid of some of its stored fats. Many fad diets rob the body of essential nutrients and cause it to cannibalize its own stored tissue proteins in order to get the amino acids it needs. This, of course, is counterproductive.

In his book, *Mega-Nutrition,* Richard A. Kunin, M.D., says that "feasting" on large meals increases fat absorption and fat synthesis up to 40 percent by increasing the amount of enzymes needed to convert the food to fat. Instead, he suggests eating small meals at frequent intervals. "It's interesting to note," he writes, "that in nature animals that nibble don't become obese." People on Cytotoxic diets often find themselves munching on small portions of food throughout the day. This is perfectly allowable and recommended for weight loss. Just be sure the foods you are eating are free of sensitive substances and that you keep them rotating.

Kunin also points out that certain micronutrients aid in the fat-burning process. "When pantothenic acid is in short supply, body fat is burned at only half its normal rate. Similarly, B_6, the amino acids and the minerals manganese and magnesium are critical in the burning of fats."

Getting out of the addiction. In one way, getting rid of food addictions can be more difficult than dealing with alcohol or drug dependencies. In another, it's easier to get out of a food addiction. It's more difficult because the alcoholic must stop drinking all alcoholic beverages if he is to break the addiction process; the junkie must stop taking all drugs; but the person addicted to foods still needs to eat! And it is possible to eliminate a food addiction and fall right into a new one by abusing and becoming sensitive to a new food. On the other hand, it's a bit easier to deal with food addictions because there is such a wide range of foods from which to choose.

The best way to keep from becoming addicted to a new food is to strictly rotate the foods remaining in your diet, which means not repeating any food more than once every four days. This is especially important in a weight-loss program, where the food dependency is strong. Carefully follow the rotation instructions in Chapter 10, and you will be assured of an addiction-free diet.

DO IT NOW

By understanding food sensitivities and eliminating those foods from your diet, you can start on a weight-loss program that won't add additional stress to your life. I know, because I've experienced it, that it can be a pleasurable experience. So don't delay. The sooner you get started, the sooner you will be able to achieve the weight that's perfect for you.

AFTERWORD

With the discovery of food sensitivities, the Cytotoxic effect has joined the ranks of other major breakthroughs in medicine. Many new doors have been opened for scientists and researchers to explore, and recognition of this phenomenon has provided a basis for many of us to rethink our drug- and surgery-oriented approaches to healing.

We have illustrated and speculated about some of our areas of research throughout the chapters of this book. Other areas are still on the horizon, but we know that white cell death caused by toxic substances entering the body as foods will soon be proven a causative factor in many of our major disease processes.

Clearly, we are at the forefront of an exciting new era in medicine, an era of reacquainting ourselves with our bodies and of understanding the inherent qualities that allow us to heal ourselves. As more people become aware of the impact on their bodies of the foods they eat and use this awareness to overcome many of their illness symptoms, we will begin to have the clinical information we need to move forward with our research and documentation.

And as scientists increasingly spend their time and energy studying the Cytotoxic phenomenon, which gratifyingly is beginning to happen, they will further unravel the work started by the likes of Dr. William T. K. Bryan and Marian Bryan, the originators of this technique; Dr. Geoffrey Cheung, head of research at Physicians Laboratories of California; and others who have dedicated their careers to food sensitivity/allergy research. These scientists will eventually solve the mysteries of the biochemical processes that cause the Cytotoxic effect.

Those of us involved in scientific research are often amazed by the irony of our explorations. Our research may be complicated, sometimes taking years or even generations before answers are formulated. And so often, after all the painstaking research and careful documentation has taken place, what we come up with is an answer so simple, so logical that we wonder why we never thought about it before.

Such has been the case in Cytotoxic testing. The biochemical processes that the body goes through are, indeed, complicated, and most of them have yet to be discovered. But what is so astonishingly simple, both in cause and in cure, is that many of our chronic illnesses, addictions, and degenerations are caused by nothing more than the foods we eat every day.

And what we researchers sheepishly admit never having given much attention to before is the factor that makes it all so elusive, yet so logical—our nutritional individuality.

Often in medicine, we tend to outsmart ourselves with an insistence on high technology answers to our medical questions. The more elaborate the procedure, the safer we feel. Happily, while there will always be a place for the amazing feats of modern medicine, we are beginning to realize that in order to cure ourselves, we must look inward and gain an understanding of our own, individual selves; exploring and ascertaining why we are reacting the way we are to certain stimuli.

It is more difficult, by far, to simplify than it is to make things more complicated, but this is exactly the challenge of the 1980s—and not only in medicine.

The research we conduct gives us the utmost respect for the inherent wisdom of our biochemical processes. It's a wisdom we are only beginning to grasp. The constant compromise, the will to survive, the full cooperation existing among all the cells of the body is a revelation and an inspiration that leads us to believe that these qualities are basic to the human condition, that these qualities are the ideals we should be striving for in every way—inward and outward.

The future of Cytotoxic research depends on our ability to reassess many of our approaches to the healing arts. And this, in no uncertain terms, is happening.

APPENDIX

WHAT'S IN WHAT YOU DRINK

Alcoholic beverages may have been manufactured from natural ingredients at one time, and to be sure, some still are. But current government regulations permit brewers to use more than seventy-five additives in their beers, and in wine making the situation is about the same. Some of these additives may be necessary and harmless, like those extracted from natural sources such as Iceland moss, maidenhair fern, poplar buds, and beechwood chips. Others are polysyllabic tongue twisters such as calcium disodium ethylenediaminetetraacetate, or heptyl para hydroxybenzoate, to name just two.

We present here, for your information, a list of ingredients that are contained in some alcoholic beverages. A complete listing is not possible at this time, since a vast majority of breweries, vintners, and distillers refuse to cooperate on any informational study. The Center for Science in the Public Interest (CSPI), a nonprofit, membership-supported organization, contacted ninety-two American alcohol beverage companies, asking for complete ingredient information on their products. Only seven provided the information. CSPI used data from the June 18, 1982, Federal Register to compile a list of additives found in wines; they used information from a March 21, 1980, Bureau of Alcohol, Tobacco and Firearms reference manual for those found in beers.

It's important to note that not all beers and wines contain all these additives. We present this information here because it's not readily available and will be of interest to anyone concerned about what they consume.

Chemicals Used in Brewing Beer

Enzymes that Convert Starch to Sugars
Proteases and carbohyrases derived from nontoxic strains of:
    Aspergillus niger
    Asperillus oryzae
    Bacillus licheniformis
    Bacillus subtilis
Carbohydrase derived from nontoxic and nonpathogenic strains of:
    Rhizopus oryzae
Bromelain
Diastase
Ficin
Papain

For Clarifying and Chill-proofing
Proteases and carbohydrases from:
    Aspergillus niger
    Aspergillus oryzae
    Bacillus subtilis
Bromelain
Ficin

For Clarifying and Chill-proofing (continued)
Papain
Pepsin
Gallotannin (Tannin)

Foam Stabilizing and Antigushing Agents
Acacia (Gum Arabic)
Alginate (Propylene Glycol Alginate)
Calcium Disodium Ethylenediaminetetraacetate
Glycerin
Peptone

Antioxidants
Sodium Ascorbate
Isoascorbates
Potassium Metabisulfate
Sodium Bisulfite
Sodium Hydrosulfite
Sodium Metabisulfite

Natural and Artificial Flavors
Benzyl Propionate
Borneol
Calcium Chloride
Citral
Citric Acid
Citronellol
Cis-3-Hexanol
Cognac Oil
Corn Syrup
Ethyl Acetate
Ethyl Acetoacetate
Ethyl Alcohol
Ethyl Butyrate
Ethyl Oenanthate (Ethyl Enanthate; Ethyl Heptanoate)
Ethyl Propionate
Ethyl Vanillin
Glycerin (Glycerol)
Grapefruit Oil
Hexanal

Natural and Artificial Flavors (continued)
Hexanol (Hexyl Alcohol)
Isoamyl Acetate
Isoamyl Alcohol
Isobutyl Alcohol
Isopulegol
Jasmine Oil
Lactic Acid
Lactose
Lemon Oil
Licorice
Lime Oil
Menthol
Methyl Anthranilate
Monosodium Glutamate
Propyl Alcohol
Quassia extract
Sodium Chloride
Sodium Citrate
Styralyl Acetate (Methylbenzyl acetate)
Sucrose
Sucrose Octaacetate
Tartaric Acid
Undecalcatone

Artificial Colors
Caramel
Enoclanina
FD & C Blue No. 1
FD & C Red No. 40
FD & C Yellow No. 5

Antimicrobial Preservative
Heptylparaben (n-heptyl p-hydroxybenzoate)

Chemicals Used In Wine Production

Acacia (Gum Arabic)
Activated carbon
Agar-agar

Chemicals Used In Wine Production (continued)
Albumin (egg white)
Ammonium Carbonate
Ammonium Hydroxide
Ammonium Phosphate

Antifoaming and Defoaming Agents
Silicon Dioxide
Sorbic Acid
Sodium Carboxymethyl Cellulose
Dimethyl Polysiloxane
Polyoxyethylene (40) Monostearate
Sorbitan Monstearate
Ascorbic Acid and Iso-Ascorbic Acid (erythorbic acid)
Autolyzed Yeast
Bentonite (Wyoming clay)
Calcium Carbonate (with and without calcium salts of tartaric
    and malic acids)
Calcium Sulfate (gypsum)
Carbon Dioxide
Casein, Potassium salt of Casein, and Milk Powder (nonfat dry
    milk)
Cellulose (food grade)
Citric Acid
Copper Sulfate
Diatomacious Earth
Glucose Oxidase and Glucose Catalase
Ferrocyanide Compounds
Ferrous Sulfate
Fumaric Acid
Gelatin
Granular Cork
Hydrogen Peroxide
Ion Exchange Resins
Isinglass
Lactic Acid
Malic Acid
Malo-lactic Bacteria
Mineral Oil
Nitrogen Gas

Antifoaming and Defoaming Agents (continued)
Charred Oak Chips
Sawdust, uncharred and untreated
Parabens
(n-alkyl esters of 4-hydroxy-benzoic acid; n-heptyl-propyl-methylparaben)
Pectolytic Enzymes
Polyvinyl-polypyrrolidone (PVPP)
Polyvinyl-pyrrolidone (PVP)
Potassium Bitartrate
Potassium Carbonate
Potassium Citrate
Potassium Metabisulfite
Propylene Glycol
Silica Gel
Soy Flour
Sulfur Dioxide
Tannin
Tartaric Acid
Urea

Chemicals Used in Spirits and Liquors

Of all alcoholic beverages, distilled spirits have the least amount of additives. The high alcohol content is sufficient to kill bacteria or yeast.

Food Substances Contained in Some Alcoholic Beverages

Beer and Ale
Malt
Rice
Hops
Yeast
Cereal grains (sometimes)
Corn sugar   "
Cornstarch   "
Corn   "
Corn grits   "

*Food Substances Contained
in Some Alcoholic Beverages* (continued)

Dextrose   "
Fish glue   "
Gelatin   "
Salt   "

Wines
Grapes or fruits
Yeast
Citric acid
Cane sugar
Egg whites
Herbs
Gelatin
Additives

Brandy and Distilled Wine
Fruit
Sugar
Caramel
Yeast
Flavorings
Clarifiers

Tequila
Maguey, a Mexican plant

Liqueurs
Whiskey or brandy or neutral spirits
Fruit products
Herbs
Spices

Spirits: Whiskey & Bourbon
Corn/cereal grains
Malt enzymes
Caramel
Yeast
Flavorings
Barley
Rye

*Food Substances Contained
in Some Alcoholic Beverages* (continued)

Gin
English: wheat
American: corn
Dutch: malt wine
   may also contain: juniper berries, sugar, aromatics

Vodka
America: corn
English: wheat
French: potato

Rum
Cane sugar/molasses
Yeast
Flavorings
Caramel
Brandy

Sake
Rice

WORKS CITED

Bosco, J. J., and Robin, S. S. "Hyperkinesis: How Common Is It and How Is It Treated?" in *Hyperactive Children: The Social Ecology of Identification and Treatment.* Edited by C. M. Whalen and B. Henker. New York: Academic, 1979.

Center for Science in the Public Interest. *Chemical Additives in Booze.* 1982.

Conners, Dr. C. Keith. *Food Additives for Hyperactive Children.* New York: Plenum Press, 1980.

Conrad, Marion L. *Allergy Cooking.* New York: Thomas Y. Crowell Co., 1960.

Cott, Dr. Allan, et al. *Fasting: A Way of Life.* New York: Bantam, 1977.

Cousins, Norman. *Anatomy of an Illness.* New York: W. W. Norton & Co., 1979.

Crook, Dr. William G. *Tracking Down Hidden Food Allergy.* Jackson, Tenn.: Professional Books, 1980.

DEHIGIA, DR. HARSHA. *The Allergy Book, a Family Guide.* New York: Contemporary Books, 1981.

EAGLE, ROBERT. *Eating and Allergy.* New York: Doubleday & Co., 1981.

FRAZIER, DR. CLAUDE. *Coping with Food Allergy: Symptoms and Treatment.* New York: Quadrangle, Books, 1974.

HUGHES DR., E. C., et al. "Attention Deficit Disorder with Hyperactivity." Study done at the University of Southern California School of Medicine, 1981.

JOHNSTONE, DR. DOUGLAS E. *The Annals of Allergy* 46 (October 1981): 225–33.

KUNIN, DR. RICHARD A. *Mega-Nutrition.* New York: McGraw-Hill, 1980.

MACDOUGALL, ROGER. "Beyond the Speculative Future." *Let's Live* magazine, May 1979.

———. Letter to *Let's Live* magazine.

———. *My Fight against Multiple Sclerosis.* London: self-published.

MANDELL, FRAN GARE. *Dr. Mandell's Allergy-Free Cookbook.* New York: Pocket Books, 1981.

MANDELL, MARSHALL, and SCANLON, LYNNE WALLER. *Dr. Mandell's Five Day Allergy Relief System.* New York: Thomas Y. Crowell Co., 1979.

NONKEN PAMELA P., and HIRSCH, DR. S. ROGER. *Allergy Cookbook and Food-Buying Guide.* New York: Warner Books, 1982.

OSAKI, DR. FRANK, and BELL, JOHN V. *Don't Drink Your Milk!* New York: Wyden Books, 1977.

PASSWATER, DR. RICHARD. *Super-Nutrition for Healthy Hearts.* New York: The Dial Press, 1977.

PHILPOTT, DR. WILLIAM H., and KALITA, DR. DWIGHT K. *Brain Allergies: The Psychonutrient Connection.* New Canaan, Conn.: Keats Publishing, 1980.

PRITIKIN, NATHAN. "Cancer and Your Diet." Paper read, March 1977.

RANDOLPH, DR. THERON G., and MOSS, DR. RALPH W. *An Alternative Approach to Allergies.* New York: Harper & Row, 1980.

RAPP, DORIS J. *Allergies and the Hyperactive Child.* New York: Cornerstone Library, 1979.

ROMBAUER, IRMA S., and BECKER, MARION ROMBAUER. *Joy of Cooking.* Indianapolis: Bobbs-Merrill, 1980.

RORVIK, DAVID. "Going Sane." *Penthouse* magazine, September 1981.

SAUNDERS, JERALDINE, and ROSS, DR. HARVEY R. *Hypoglycemia: The Disease Your Doctor Won't Treat.* New York: Pinnacle Books, 1980.

SCHAUSS, ALEXANDER. *Diet, Crime and Delinquency.* Berkeley, Calif.: Parker House Publishing Co., 1970.

SELYE, DR. HANS. *The Stress of Life.* New York: McGraw-Hill, 1956.

SINACORE, J. S. *Health: A Quality of Life.* New York: Macmillan, 1968.

SMITH, DR. LENDON. *Foods for Healthy Kids.* New York: McGraw-Hill, 1981.

U.S. Government Printing Office. *Recommended Daily Allowances.* 8th edition. Washington, D.C., 1974.

WALFORD, DR. ROY L. *Maximum Life Span.* New York: W. W. Norton & Co., 1983.

WILLIAMS, ROGER J. *Physicians' Handbook of Nutritional Science.* Springfield, Ill.: Charles C. Thomas, 1978.